Arthur Penrhyn Stanley

Addresses and sermons, delivered during a visit to the United States and Canada in 1878

Arthur Penrhyn Stanley

Addresses and sermons, delivered during a visit to the United States and Canada in 1878

ISBN/EAN: 9783337208486

Printed in Europe, USA, Canada, Australia, Japan

Cover: Foto ©ninafisch / pixelio.de

More available books at **www.hansebooks.com**

ADDRESSES AND SERMONS,

DELIVERED DURING A VISIT

TO THE UNITED STATES AND CANADA

IN 1878.

BY

ARTHUR PENRHYN STANLEY, D.D.

Dean of Westminster.

THIRD EDITION.

New York:
MACMILLAN & CO.
1881.

PREFACE.

I HAVE been asked by my kind friends in America to leave with them a record of the utterances which, whether in the reception of their generous hospitalities or in the more solemn form of addresses from the pulpit, have been drawn from me during my brief journey through the United States and Canada. It will be evident that the speeches delivered on the social occasions which led to them were sometimes entirely unpremeditated, and always deficient in that preparation which I could have wished. But as they truly expressed, in however imperfect a form, the feelings inspired by the new experiences with which my rapid survey of American life for the first time brought me into contact, I have not scrupled to recall them. Some of these are reproduced from the reports, more or less exact, of the American journals. In two instances (the addresses to the

Episcopal Clergy of Boston and of New York) no report was given, and what is here printed can but represent the substance so far as it was retained by memory.

The Addresses, as will be seen, were delivered to very various audiences, some of them consisting chiefly of the great communions of the Presbyterians, Congregationalists, Methodists, and Baptists, which have played so large a part in the religious development of the American people. The Sermons, on the other hand, were all delivered in the Protestant Episcopal Church. The limitations of time were of themselves quite sufficient to preclude any attempt at wider ministrations, and the liberality with which the various sections of that Church offered to me the opportunity of speaking from its pulpits to the people of America, rendered any further effort unnecessary.

Two additions I have ventured to make to the Sermons preached in the United States. One is that which was delivered in the Cathedral of Quebec. The common interest which attaches to the whole Northern Continent will enable the reader to enter into the grateful farewell which that Sermon was intended to express to the departing Governor, who has done so much for Canada, as well as the respectful greeting to the coming Governor, from whose peculiar vantage-ground so much is expected. I have also added, as a preface to the whole collection of Sermons, the substance of one preached in England, which indicates in a more systematic form than was possible in these discourses the general conditions of religious inquiry, applicable equally to the theological students of both countries. It also bears directly on the subject of the two last discourses in New York.

I commend these pages to the indulgence of the American public, with the humble hope that they may tend in some measure to forward those higher principles of Christian civilisation, on which the future progress alike of the British Empire and of the United States so largely depends.

TABLE OF CONTENTS.

ADDRESSES :
               PAGE
 SALEM—"OUR OLD HOMES" 3
 BOSTON—LIBERAL THEOLOGY 8
 BALTIMORE—JOHNS HOPKINS UNIVERSITY. . . 16
 IRVINGTON.—REPLY TO THE REV. DR. ADAMS . . 19
 NEW YORK—AN AMERICAN SCHOLAR . . . 23
   ,, JOHN WESLEY 34
   ,, REPLY AT THE CENTURY CLUB . . 49
   ,, REPLY TO THE BAPTIST MINISTERS . 56
   ,, THE PROSPECTS OF THE CHURCH OF
       ENGLAND 60

SERMONS :
 PREFACE—ON THE CONDITIONS OF RELIGIOUS INQUIRY 71
 BOSTON—THE EAST AND THE WEST 96
 PHILADELPHIA—THE HOLY ANGELS 115
 NEW YORK—THE PERPLEXITIES OF LIFE . . . 133
 QUEBEC—THE USES OF CONFLICT 151
 STOCKBRIDGE, MASS.—"THERE IS NOTHING" . . 172
 NEW YORK—THE UNITY AND DIVERSITY OF
      CHRISTENDOM 184
   ,, THE NATURE OF MAN 200
   ,, THE NATURE OF GOD 228

ADDRESSES

ADDRESSES.

I.

SPEECH IN REPLY TO THE TOAST OF "OUR OLD HOMES,"

AT THE BANQUET AT SALEM, MASSACHUSETTS, SEPT. 19, 1878, ON THE OCCASION OF THE TWO HUNDRED AND FIFTIETH ANNIVERSARY OF THE LANDING OF GOVERNOR ENDICOTT.

Mr. President: You are aware that I have been but two days on this side of the Atlantic. I came to this country not to speak but to hear, not to teach but to learn, and therefore you will not expect me, even if there were not more potent reasons, to address you at present at any length. But, after the kind way in which you have proposed my health, after the kind reception with which I have been met, after the tribute which I feel is given in my humble honour to my own country, I cannot refrain from a few words to express the deep gratification which I have had at being present, under the kind protection of my ancient friend, Mr. Winthrop, and my new friend, the Governor of Massachusetts, on this auspicious occasion. You propose "our old homes." Our old homes. It has often struck me that I should almost have wished to have been born on this side of the Atlantic, as a citizen of the United States, in order to have felt the pleasure which I have seen again and again in the faces of Americans as they have witnessed their old homes on the other side of the ocean. It has been my constant happiness to receive them in that oldest of all the old homes, whether of Old England or New England, Westminster Abbey. It is a pleasure to me to think that those who cross from this side of the Atlantic may find something in that old home which may remind them of their new homes here. You may see on the walls of Westminster Abbey a tablet, placed in that church by the State of Massachusetts itself, in that dubious period over which the eloquent orator of to-day passed with so tender and delicate a step. And you will see the temporary grave of your illustrious townsman, the munificent benefactor of the poor of

London, where his remains were placed amidst the mourning of the whole metropolis. You will even see in a corner there, most sacred of memory, Boston harbour depicted with the sun setting behind the western world.

But as there is a pleasure which Americans feel in visiting their old home, there is a pleasure which an Englishman feels when, after long waiting and long desiring, he visits for the first time the shores of this new home of his old race. You can hardly imagine the intense curiosity with which, as he enters Boston harbour, he sees the natural features opening upon his view, of which he has so long read in books, and when he sees pointed out to him name after name familiar in his own country. And when I come to this celebration, cold and hard must be the heart of that Englishman who would not feel drawn to a place hallowed by the recollection of those Puritan fathers whose ancestors were as valuable an element in our society as they can have been in yours. Long, long ago, before I had formed the design of coming to America, I had been drawn to the city of Salem as the birthplace of one whom I may call my friend, the gifted sculptor, whose vigorous and vivid poem we all heard with so much pleasure to-day, and also as the cradle of the genius ranking amongst the first places of the literature of this age and country, the genius of Nathaniel Hawthorne.

And listening to all the marvellous strains of interest which have gone through the speeches of this day, one point which strikes me most forcibly is that I am carried back from these shores to my own country two hundred and fifty years ago. I doubt whether there is any audience in England which could be equally impressed by any event that had taken place in England two hundred and fifty years ago, with the feeling toward the mother country and toward the societies of their own country which I have seen throughout the proceedings of to-day. The foundation of Salem is indeed an event which unites together our old and our new homes, and if there is a mixture of light and shade in the recollections which crowd upon us, that also is important in its relation to the future development of our race. If in Salem we stand on the grave of some extinct beliefs—extinct and vanished away, as we trust, for ever—so in Salem we cannot but look forward to that distant future, to the ages in which no one can forecast with any certainty the destinies either of Europe or America, but in which we still hope that our own

English race may, under the providence of God, effect new works and fulfil new hopes for the human race, such as, perhaps, at present we hardly dare think of—

'Tis not too late to seek a newer world.

II.

THE PROSPECTS OF LIBERAL THEOLOGY.

THE SUBSTANCE OF A REPLY AT A RECEPTION OF THE CLERGY OF THE PROTESTANT EPISCOPAL CHURCH OF MASSACHUSETTS AND RHODE ISLAND, AT BOSTON, SEPTEMBER 23, 1878.

You have asked me to give a brief account of the prospects of Liberal Theology in England. It is not altogether a view of unmixed rejoicing. During the last thirty years there have been many reverses, on which I will not dwell. Still, there have been successes achieved which justify us in hoping that, if not now, at any rate years or generations hence, Liberal Theology may resume its natural ascendency over the minds of educated men. By Liberal Theology, I mean a theology which, whilst comprehending all the wholesome elements of thought at work in the world, yet holds that the Christian belief is large enough to contain them; which insists not on the ceremonial, the dogmatic, or the portentous, but on the moral side of religion; which insists on the spirit, not on the letter—on the meaning, not on the words—on the progressive, not on the stationary character of Christianity.

Let me take four groups of instances in which the public opinion of the clergy has been deeply changed in this direction even during the last few years.

(1.) First, as regards the Bible. The crude notions which prevailed twenty years ago on the subject of inspiration have been so completely abandoned, as to be hardly anywhere maintained by theological scholars. Of the eleven thousand English clergy who set their hands to a declaration in favour of those crude notions fifteen years ago, there are probably not fifty who would now do it again.

As regards the interpretation of the sacred books, questions of criticism and authorship which were formerly considered to be entirely closed are now fully and freely discussed. The non-Pauline authorship of the Epistle to the Hebrews, which thirty years ago is said to have excluded a candidate from a theological professorship, is now maintained by no one of any name or fame. The second Isaiah, if not equally recognised, can be at any rate mentioned without exciting alarm or scandal. The composite character of the Pentateuch, in like manner, on which the Bishop of Natal found such extraordinary difficulty in obtaining a patient hearing, is now, in principle, assumed almost as certain. The complexity of the mutual relation of the four Gospels, although still agitated, without arriving, as perhaps we never shall arrive, at any fixed solution, is yet so deeply impressed on the theological mind that no scholar can for the future avoid considering it. The Biblical criticism, begun so admirably at Oxford by Professor Jowett, and continued in a more cautious spirit, though with more visible results, at Cambridge, by Professor Lightfoot, is full of promise for the future.

(2.) Secondly, as regards social and ecclesiastical questions. In spite of the retrograde influences which have prevailed within or without the Church, it may be safely asserted that never has the Liberal doctrine of the relations of Church and State been more thoroughly ventilated than in these later years. The doctrine laid down by Hooker, which has always more or less animated the policy of enlightened statesmen and divines in England, received a new elucidation in the writings of Arnold, and has on the whole successfully held its ground. If the Church of England perishes, it will not be, as might have been the case forty years ago, for want of a thoroughly reasonable and philosophical vindication of the principles of a National Church. The good relations between Churchmen and Nonconformists, though they have lost much, have also gained much. The admission of the Dissenters to the universities, their association with the revision of the translation of the Bible, are points which, once achieved, will not be surrendered.

(3.) Our dogmatical expositions have undergone a modification so extensive, as that probably no treatise on any of them would now be written with the phraseology current forty years ago. The doctrine of the Atonement will never again appear in the crude form common both in Protestant and Roman Catholic churches in former times. The doctrine of the more merciful view of future punishment, and of the hope of a universal restitution, has been gradually advancing, and the darker view gradually receding. The doctrine of the Trinity has been more and more resolved into its Biblical character; the Athanasian creed, by half of the English clergy has been condemned, and by the Irish Church has been silenced;

and though there are many who insist on retaining the old repulsive scholastic forms, the main stumbling-blocks involved in them have lost their general interest. The quarrels about Predestination and Justification, which a hundred years ago filled the whole mind of the Scottish and English Nonconformists, have, even with them, almost disappeared. The question of miracles has at least reached this point—that no one would now make them the chief or sole basis of the evidence for religious truth. In this intermediate position the contending parties may surely rest for a time.

In all these and many like respects, Liberal Theology, instead of standing on the merely apologetic ground of defending itself against the attacks of its assailants, ought itself to claim an orthodoxy (if we like so to call it), a Biblical, Evangelical, Catholic character, which its opponents have never reached. On many of the essential doctrines of Christianity, the universality of the Divine Love, the justification of the good heathens, the supreme importance of morality, the possibility of human perfection, the divinity of conscience, the identification of the Church with the laity, of things secular and things sacred, the Bible and the best voices of Christendom are on our side and not on theirs; and though, on account of the many-sidedness of truth, and the imperfection of human language, there is much to be forgiven on both sides, yet, on the whole, it is they, not we, whose extravagances need to be tolerated, and whose errors need to be condoned.

(4.) The general relations of Theology to Literature have gained immensely. In ecclesiastical history, Milman and Lecky, with many lesser works on special periods, have admirably filled the waste places. Tennyson's poems and Max Müller's researches are a storehouse of wise theology. With all the objections that may be made to Matthew Arnold, he has—in his father's spirit, though in a different direction—left an enduring mark in the light he has thrown not only on the controversy with Puritans, but on the importance of the Bible, and in the call to every theological formula to cast off its provincial and scholastic form and take the literary and universal form, which is the test of ultimate permanence.

One word in conclusion. Whatever the relapses to which I referred at the beginning of these remarks, whatever the failures in store for us in the future, I am persuaded that what is called Liberal Theology is the backbone of the Church of England, and will be found to be the backbone of its daughter Church in America. The fact that a large portion of the world and the Church is against us ought not to alter our conviction that, in the main, we are right. We must still hold by our colours. We have made good a starting-point for those who come after us, perhaps in the twentieth or the twenty-first century, and no deeper impression will have been left upon this age than by those who have followed in the broad track opened by the great philosophic divines of the seventeenth century; an impress, it may be, all the deeper, even if, which I do not venture to anticipate, it shall come to pass that we shall be remembered as the last of the Liberal Theologians, the last of those who in England did not despair of their religion and their Church.

Of your future in America, it is not for me to speak. Any stranger who comes to your country for the first time must be awestruck by the vastness of the destiny before it. But, perhaps, he may be allowed to express his hopes in the form of an earnest entreaty that you, the clergy, will remember the greatness of your profession—great in itself, and great in its relation to the other churches and communions around you; that you will remember how much of that greatness belongs to the large and liberal conceptions of Christianity which, in America as well as in England, and in New England especially, have been breathed into your minds by the genial influences of the earlier part of this century.

When I see hereafter in Westminster Abbey the memorial which in its most beloved spot contains a faint representation of Boston harbour, when I listen there once more, as I trust I shall, to the eloquent voice which I have already twice heard within those walls, and now, with renewed pleasure, in Trinity Church, the scenes of this first welcome to your shores will recur with delight to my thoughts. May the grateful sense of the kindness which I have received from you shape itself into the sincere prayer that God may bless you with the fulness of His blessing.

III.

ADDRESS

AT AN EVENING MEETING OF THE STUDENTS OF THE JOHNS HOPKINS UNIVERSITY, BALTIMORE, SEPTEMBER 30, 1878.

I AM no speaker, but I must return a few words of thanks for the kind language with which I have been received. When I see an institution like this in its first beginnings, I am carried back to the time when my own university in England was begun, perhaps a thousand years ago, in the fabulous obscurity of the age of Alfred, or the more recent historic times of Walter of Merton or Devorguilla of Balliol; and I observe the repetition of the same yearnings after a distant future of improvement, as those which were before the minds of those old mediæval founders. The same spirit is needed for that improvement on this side of the ocean and on the other. I am led to think of the description given by Chaucer, in that inestimable Prologue to the Canterbury Tales, which I hope you will all read one day or other, of the Good Scholar and the Good Pastor, bred in Oxford in his time; and I see how, in spite of all the vast changes which have passed over the minds of men since that age, the same qualities are still necessary to make a good and sincere scholar, a good scientific student, an efficient medical or legal adviser, an efficient spiritual pastor. Simplicity, sincerity, love of goodness, and love of truth, are as powerful and as much needed in our day as they were in the days long ago, which formed the great professions that are still the bulwarks of society. The President and the Professor who have spoken have both referred to the influence of my beloved teacher in former times—Thomas Arnold. The lapse of years has only served to deepen in me the conviction that no gift can be more valuable than the recollection and the inspiration of a great character working upon our own. It is my hope that you may all experience this at some time of your lives as I have done. I entreat you to cherish this hope, and to remember that on your making the best of any such influences, and also of the remarkable resources provided for you in this noble institution, depends your use in life and the effect which you may produce on the future generations of this great country. There are many evils, many difficulties, individual and national, with which you will have to contend; but it may possibly cheer you in your efforts to recall these words of an Englishman who now sees you for the first time, and who will in all probability never see you again. May God bless you all.

IV.

REPLY TO A SPEECH OF THE REV. DR. ADAMS,

President of the Presbyterian Union Seminary at New York,

AT THE HOUSE OF CYRUS W. FIELD, ESQ., IRVINGTON, ON THE HUDSON, OCTOBER 8, 1878.

THERE is one criticism which Dr. Adams's kind words suggest to my mind—namely, that Americans are inclined to believe that Englishmen have the same extraordinary fluency of speech that they have themselves. But there is one consolation. When on the eve of starting for America, I said to a young Englishman who had visited this country that my heart almost sank at the prospect of so long and difficult a journey, and I asked him, "What do you think is the chief pleasure of travelling in America?"

He said: "The pleasure in travelling there is being in a foreign country, and yet being able to talk in our own language." It is so. I feel that, however difficult it is to attempt to make a speech in English to Americans, it would be much more difficult if I had to do so in bad French or worse Spanish. The relation between the two countries has not only been cemented by the cable—of which there are so many natural mementoes in this house—but also by this intercommunity of sentiment and speech. As has been said by Keble:

> Brothers are brothers evermore;
> No distance breaks the tie of blood.

You remember the beautiful classical legend of Arethusa plunging into the sea, and coming up again in the form of the fountain at Syracuse; which was a sign that although the colonists of that city had bidden a final adieu to their parent city in Greece, they had not forgotten that they were the same people under a different sky. I have already found, while travelling here, in every city and town I visit, under every hill and in every stream, such springs of Arethusa breaking forth and welcoming me. Your Washington Irving, whose home was here in this neighbourhood, and whose tomb is among you, is still, we may consider, in Westminster Abbey, where Poets' Corner not only comprises those whose bodies lie there, but also in a wider sense the distant poets and authors who lie elsewhere. He was the first American who spoke of that venerable building with the fond respect which has now become part of yourselves; he was among the first to create that feeling of affection between England and your own country after the great separation, which must still grow with the growth of years, and make the two nations one in feeling, in affection, and in hope for future advancement.

There seems to me nothing more foolish than for strangers hastily to express opinions upon problems that can only be settled by yourselves. But one word I may say. You are still young, and will have all the difficulties forced upon you that we have encountered. You will, however, have the advantage of the experience of our past ages to assist you in overcoming them. The conditions of our two countries are so different that each must judge charitably of each other. There are, perhaps, no Scotsmen here, but all Presbyterians understand Scotch, and will appretiate what an old minister of the Church of Scotland said to a young Scottish Dissenter who was full of complaints: "When your lum (chimney) has reeked as long as ours, perhaps it will have as much soot;" and I hope that your chimney-sweepers may be as effective as ours have been. May God's blessing rest upon all endeavours to bring together our different Churches in unity of spirit, however parted in form.

V.

AN AMERICAN SCHOLAR.

AN ADDRESS TO THE STUDENTS* OF THE UNION THEOLOGICAL SEMINARY OF THE PRESBYTERIAN CHURCH OF AMERICA, AT THE SEMINARY IN NEW YORK, OCT. 29, 1878.

IT gives me great pleasure, not only to hear the kind words of your President, but to see the faces of so many young students, who are called to work in this seminary and to carry out in their several spheres the destinies, so far as in them lies, of the Church to which they belong and of the vast Republic of which that Church forms so large a part. Your President has spoken of the contrast between the youth of this country and the age of mine. That, of course, is a contrast which strikes everyone who comes from the other side of the Atlantic to this; but there is one element which is common to both sides of the Atlantic

---

* This Address is printed almost *verbatim* from an unusually faithful report made by the students themselves.

one spring of youth which is perpetual, and that is the sight of the young generation rising up and the inspiration which that sight gives to anyone who looks upon them. I remember a friend* of mine, a poet, who has visited America, and whose name is dear to both countries, once quoting those lines of Wordsworth's,

> My heart leaps up when I behold
> A rainbow in the sky;

" and," he added—we were speaking about colleges—" my heart leaps up when I behold an undergraduate." Well, that is very much my feeling when I look upon you. Young men all over the world are very much the same; and what I would say to young men at Oxford or Cambridge I believe I may fairly say to you.

I would wish, as far as I can, to concentrate my remarks, so as not to lose myself in those vague commonplaces into which one is liable to fall when speaking in the midst of an institution of which one knows very little, and to persons who of necessity are strangers. This I will endeavour to effect by recalling to you and to myself a debt of gratitude which for many, many years I have owed to Union Seminary.

---

* The late Arthur H. Clough.

My first acquaintance with American theological literature—I might almost say my first exact acquaintance with American literature at all—was in reading the works of a Professor of Union Seminary. I mean the "Biblical Researches" of Dr. Robinson. Whether any of you have ever embarked on the study of those four volumes it is not for me to ask; but they are amongst the very few books of modern literature of which I can truly say that I have read every word. I have read them under circumstances which riveted my attention upon them (though, no doubt, not conducive to a very profound study of them)—while riding on the back of a camel in the Desert; while travelling on horseback through the hills of Palestine; under the shadow of my tent, when I came in weary from the day's journey. These were the scenes in which I first became acquainted with the work of Dr. Robinson. But to that work I have felt that I and all students of Biblical literature owe a debt that never can be effaced. Those books are not such as any theological student in America, or elsewhere, will be likely to read through unless he has some special stimulus to do so. But I cannot help recalling them on this occasion, not only for the special personal reason which I have mentioned, but also because they appear to me to furnish a kind of framework for some remarks which are applicable to all theological students everywhere.

There are three characteristics of the "Biblical Researches" of Dr. Robinson which apply far more widely than to the study of sacred geography. The first is the devotion with which he applied himself to one particular portion of the study of the Bible—the outer framework of it—without any fear or hesitation as to any consequences which might be derived from it. Dr. Robinson, I believe it is not too much to say, was the first person who ever saw Palestine with his eyes open as to what he ought to see. Hundreds and thousands of travellers had visited Palestine before—pilgrims, seekers after pleasure, even scientific travellers—but there was no person before his time who had come to visit that sacred country, with all the appliances ready beforehand which were necessary to enable him to understand what he saw; and he also was the first person who came there with an eye capable of observing, and a hand capable of recording, all that with these appliances he brought before his vision. Now, this is a part of his work which applies to many other subjects than to the geography of Palestine or the geography of Arabia. It is the same principle which I endeavour to impress upon all theological students—the great difference between having eyes to observe and not having eyes to observe. You may travel through a country; you may travel through a book; you may travel through the Bible itself, either with eyes to see what is in that book or in that land, or with the dull, unreasoning, unobserving blindness which sees nothing at all. You ought to cultivate as much as possible this habit of observation. You ought to cultivate it, I say, without fear of the consequences. There are some people who, I believe, are afraid even of sacred geography. They are afraid of having the outward facts and circumstances connected with sacred history brought close to them. I remember hearing of an old Scotswoman—no doubt an old Scottish Presbyterian—who, on being told that some one had been to Jerusalem, said: "You will na make me believe that. There is na such place as Jerusalem on airth!" Well, that feeling of the old Scotswoman is, I believe, very common with a large part of the community. They cannot bring themselves to believe that the events of which we read in the Bible really occurred amongst persons like ourselves; and it is one great advantage of such a faithful, accurate study of Palestine as Dr. Robinson gave to us, that we are almost forced to remember that such is the case—that there was a real geography; there was a real history; there were real men and women, who are described in the Old and New Testaments, and whom we must approach with all reverence and with all humility, but still with the firm conviction that they lived in the same humble kind of way, and with the same human passions and infirmities, or at least with the same outward surroundings as ourselves.

The second lesson which I would wish you to derive from this work of your celebrated Professor is this :—

A friend of mine, at Oxford, once paid a visit to a very old man, who was regarded as a kind of oracle, for he lived to his hundredth year; and the longer he lived the more people went to inquire of him, as if he were an infallible oracle. My friend went to him, and said : "Would you kindly give me some advice in regard to reading theology?" And he was rather discomfited at the old man's saying, after a long pause : "I will give you my advice. It is, *Verify your references.*" Well, I will not confine myself to so homely a piece of advice as that, although it was very good; but I will say : *Verify your facts.* That was what Professor Robinson did, with the greatest care. One value of his book on Palestine is its extreme accuracy. I travelled with those four volumes through the country, and at the end of the time I wrote to him at New York, to say that the greatest compliment that I could pay him, after having read his books under such circumstances, was that I had found in them only three small, insignificant errors. This accuracy, this verification of facts, this sifting of things to the bottom, is a thing which all students ought to cultivate, and which theological students ought especially to cultivate, because it is something which theological students are especially apt to neglect. Do let me entreat of you to look facts in the face, whether the facts of the Bible, or the facts of science, or the facts of scholarship. Do not be afraid of them. Go as far as you possibly can in the language of Greek and Hebrew, in the comparison of the sacred volumes of the Old and New Testaments with the sacred volumes of other religions. Make the most thorough and searching investigation that you can, with light from whatever quarter, as to the origin of the sacred books: and in this way you will be discharging your duty, as students and as pastors, to your Church and to your country, in this great and stirring age in which our lot is cast.

The third characteristic which distinguishes Dr. Robinson's writings is this: I have said that they are books which we are not likely to read through for ourselves, unless under some special temptation to study sacred geography; but there is one characteristic of them which we may all take as lessons to ourselves — that is, their style. The style of Dr. Robinson's book is characterised by its extreme simplicity, combined with an elevation of description and of feeling whenever the subject demands it. There are books on theology which we sometimes read, where, first of all, there is no style at all, and also where whatever style there be is all couched in the same uniform tone, either of dulness or of exaggeration. Now in Dr. Robinson's book there may be pages, no doubt, which we should call dull, because they never rise above the actual facts which he has to teach us; but whenever he does come within sight of some great and impressive scene—when he comes, for example, within sight of Mount Sinai or within sight of Jerusalem—his style, simple and massive as it is, is adorned with a native eloquence which at once arrests our attention and calls forth our admiration. It is this style—this union of simplicity where simplicity is desirable, and of elevation where elevation is desirable—which produces upon our minds that sense of proportion so difficult for theological students to obtain, so distinctive yet so important, whether as regards writing or preaching. To write on all sorts of subjects connected with religion in a high-flown, inflated, exaggerated manner is, as I said just now, a temptation into which we are all apt to fall. The subject rather encourages it. The subjects of theology are so great that we imagine that if we adopt this kind of exaggerated style we are only following the natural expressions of a religious heart. Nevertheless, whatever excuses we may make for this inflation, it is a thing to be especially avoided, and it is a fault into which American students of theology are especially likely to fall. Do beware of it. It very much diminishes your influence. This inflated style is really one of the chief drawbacks which we have in Europe to our enjoyment of American literature. Dr. Robinson I venture to say, is a most admirable exception, and he should be an example and a warning equally in Europe and in America.

But it is not only thus with regard to your style. It is also very desirable to keep before your minds the necessity of distinguishing between what is important and what is unimportant, what is essential and what is unessential, what is primary and what is secondary. I once knew a very distinguished Italian layman who said that, if he were to sum up the faults of the theology of the Roman Church in one word, it would be that they confounded the instrumentals with the fundamentals. There are times when we likewise are prone to confound instrumentals with fundamentals; to confound things which are of no importance at all with things which are of the utmost importance.

These are some of the remarks which have been suggested to me by finding myself confronted with so many young students, and by my having to speak in Union Seminary, which numbered Dr. Robinson among its professors. I cannot hope that remarks thrown out in this cursory and fugitive manner can produce any very lasting impression on those who hear them; yet it is possible that even remarks like these, coming from a stranger like myself, coming from one whose office, at any rate, as your President has kindly observed, is well known to you; whose habitation is connected, as he has reminded you, with the first beginnings of the theology of English, Scottish, and American Presbyterianism—may now and then recur to you in the course of your theological studies, and may lead you, perchance, into some of the reflections which I have suggested: first, on the desirableness of remembering the historical character of the sacred books with which we have to deal; secondly, on the necessity of verifying and pursuing to the utmost all facts that are brought before you, whether in science or religion; and, thirdly, the importance of observing a sense of proportion, whether in your style, or your ideas, or your conception of the various doctrines of Christianity.

I wish you all every success in the work in which you are employed. Every student and pastor has his part to play in this age of transition through which we are passing. I shall not live to see the end of those problems which now agitate the minds of men, but you will perhaps live to see them solved. You, perhaps, in the twentieth century, will live to see a brighter and a happier day than that which sometimes seems to overcloud the minds and oppress the hopes of those who live in the latter part of this nineteenth century. But I will not depart from you except with words of hope. May God bless you; may God sustain you in your efforts; may God enable you, through the spirit of wisdom and understanding and godly fear, both in your studies and in your pastoral duties, to fulfil the work, whatever it be, that He has assigned both to the greatest and the humblest amongst you.

VI.

JOHN WESLEY.

AN ADDRESS DELIVERED AT A RECEPTION BY THE BISHOPS, PASTORS, AND MEMBERS OF THE METHODIST EPISCOPAL CHURCH, IN ST. PAUL'S METHODIST CHURCH, NEW YORK, NOVEMBER 1, 1878.*

BISHOPS, PASTORS, AND MEMBERS OF THE METHODIST EPISCOPAL CHURCH : I tender to you my sincere and grateful thanks for the honour which you have done to me, and to the Church and country which I humbly represent, by the kindness and cordiality with which you have welcomed me this evening.

I am aware that one of the chief grounds—I may say the chief ground—on which this welcome has been afforded me is a recognition of the debt which I have been thankful to have been able to repay to the founder of. the Society of Methodists. When I

---

* Taken almost *verbatim* from the excellent report in *The Christian Advocate.*

think of this vast assemblage, when I think of the magnificent results which Methodism has achieved in this great country, it would be tempting to me to enlarge on the hopes and the prospects which may lie before the Methodist Church in the United States of America; but I feel that the ignorance under which a stranger comes to a foreign land forbids him to enlarge on a field of which he must necessarily know very little, and I therefore prefer to confine the few remarks which I venture to make on this occasion to the reasons which induced me in England, and which now induce me here, to pay my humble tribute to John Wesley, the founder of this great society. In so doing I trust that you will feel, and I feel myself, that I am best enlarging on the sources of your strength, and best unfolding the hopes that open before you.

In the address which has been kindly presented to me, allusion has been made to the monument in Westminster Abbey, which by my permission was erected to the memory of the two illustrious brothers who established the first beginnings of Methodism. It was some eight or ten years ago that the then President of the Wesleyan Conference in England, whose name, has been rightly mentioned in the address just read asked, with that courtesy and modesty which is characteristic of him, if I would allow the erection of a monument in Westminster Abbey, in Poets' Corner, to Charles Wesley, as the sweet Psalmist of our English Israel. I ventured to answer: "If we are to have a monument to Charles, why not to John?" To John Wesley, accordingly, together with his brother Charles — not as excluding Charles, but as the greater genius, as the greater spirit of the two — that monument has been erected. It was erected close to a monument which in the last century was placed there to the memory of the great Congregational divine and poet, Isaac Watts, and I mention the circumstance as showing that, in welcoming this recognition of your illustrious founder, I have been but following precedents already established in Westminster Abbey and in the Church of England.

It has been said in the address, and I think that it has been said also by the other speakers, that we are assembled here in a building consecrated to the Methodist worship, consecrated to the worship of Almighty God, as set on foot in this country by John Wesley. It reminds me of what happened to myself when on visiting, in London, the City Road Chapel, in which John Wesley ministered, and the cemetery adjoining in which he is buried, I asked an old man who showed me the cemetery—I asked him, perhaps inadvertently and as an English Churchman might naturally ask—"By whom was this cemetery consecrated?" and he answered: "It was consecrated by the bones of that holy man, that holy servant of God, John Wesley." In the spirit of that remark I return to the point to which I have ventured to address my remarks, and that is the claims which the character and career of John Wesley have, not only upon your veneration, but upon the veneration of English Christendom.

And first of all, may I venture to say that in claiming him as your founder, you enjoy a peculiar privilege among the various communions which have from time to time broken off from the communion of the Church of England. The founder of the English Baptists (they will allow me to say so) is comparatively unknown. The founder of the English Congregationalists (and I say it with no shadow of disrespect) is also comparatively unknown; the founder of English Unitarianism (and I say it again without a shadow of disrespect) is also comparatively obscure; the founder of the Society of Friends, George Fox, has been superseded in celebrity by William Penn, and by other illustrious Friends who have risen in that society since his departure. But it is no disrespect to the famous society of Methodists, it is no disrespect to the eminent and reverend persons who sit around me, to say that no one has risen in the Methodist Society equal to their founder, John Wesley. It is this which makes his character and his fortunes so peculiarly interesting to the whole Christian world.

And let me ask in what particulars it is that John Wesley has attained this great pre-eminence? First of all, there is a remark which is to all reflecting persons specially instructive, that, if you will allow me to say so, his career is a vindication of the character of the much despised eighteenth century. I know not whether in America, but certainly in England, it has been the habit of our time to disparage altogether the religious genius of that age. John Wesley, if any person of the last century, was a representative of it; in his long and eventful life he covered almost the whole of those hundred years. He showed that even in that century, in many respects dry and dull, there was a capacity for producing a religious character of the highest order. He was the chief reviver of religious fervour in all Protestant Churches both of the Old and the New World. He had—as has been well said by one whom I venture to call the first of modern English* critics—he had "a genius for godliness."

Again, there is this very interesting peculiarity of John Wesley—interesting not only to Wesleyans, but to every communion throughout the world—that he showed how it was possible to make a very wide divergence from the communion to which he belonged without parting from it. "I vary," he used to say, "I vary from the Church of England, but I will never leave it." And in this assurance of his determination to hold to the Church of England in spite of all difficulties and obstacles he persevered unto the end. It would be unfitting and unbecoming in me to cast any censure on the course which this great society, especially in America, has taken since his death. Circumstances change; opportunities are lost; events which might have been possible in his lifetime may have become impossible since. Nevertheless, the relations which he himself maintained towards the Church of England give encouragement to all intelligent minds and active hearts in their several communions to endeavour to make the best of an institution so long as they can possibly remain in it. And on these relations which he encouraged his fol-

---

* Matthew Arnold.

lowers to maintain, of friendliness and communion with the Church of England, I need not repeat his oft-reiterated phrases. Those expressions, those entreaties, which he urged upon his followers, not to part from the mother Church, are not the less instructive nor the less applicable because, as I have said, circumstances both in England and in America have in some degree parted us asunder. There are those in our own country—there are possibly those in America—who think that the Wesleyans, the Methodists, may perchance be one of the links of union between the mother Church of England and those who are more or less estranged from it. On this I pronounce no opinion. I know that separations once made are very difficult to reconcile. Like the two friends described by the English poet (I apply a quotation used by Norman M'Leod on a like occasion):

> They stand aloof, the scars remaining,
> Like cliffs that have been rent asunder.

But still we may always trust that something of the old affection to the old Church still continues. One cannot help seeing—this very occasion shows it—that there is something in the hearts of Methodists which responds to the feeling still entertained towards them by the mother Church. I always feel that some injustice has been done, in common parlance, both in our Church and in the outlying communions, to the bishops and the authorities of our Church at the time of John Wesley's career. It was not, as has been often incorrectly said, by the action of the English bishops that John Wesley and his followers were estranged from us. The King (George II.), the judges, and the chief bishops — I particularly mention Archbishop Potter, Bishop Gibson, Bishop Benson, and the famous Bishop Lowth—treated him with the utmost consideration and respect; and nothing could have been more friendly than the conduct of George II., or of the judges of England, toward John Wesley and his followers. It was the ignorant country squires, and country clergy, and above all the ignorant multitudes, that would not endure him. The hostility arose very much from that stupid, vulgar, illiterate prejudice which exists in the professional fanaticism and exclusiveness of the less educated clergy everywhere, and in that barbarous intolerance so characteristic of the mobs of all countries. The feeling which drove the followers of John Wesley from a place in the Church of England, a few years later drove the philosopher Priestley from his scientific studies at Birmingham to take refuge in Pennsylvania. Therefore, I repeat, the feeling between the Church of England and the Methodists need never be broken. You may remain apart from us, and we may remain apart from you; but we shall always feel that there is an undercurrent of sympathy on which we can always rely, and which, in times far distant, may possibly once more bring us together.

I pass from these preliminary and general remarks to three points which characterise the method of his teachings, and which also are of immense value for all Christian Churches.

One of them is that which is inscribed on his monument: "The world is my parish." It is true that there is a counter principle, no less true, "The parish is my world." The particular sphere in which each of us has to labour is for each of us the most important, may be for each of us the world, the chief world, perhaps the only world in which we may hope to do any good; if we fail there, we shall hardly succeed anywhere. But still we must also bear in mind Wesley's principle. We are not confined in our ministrations or our teachings only to the particular sphere in which our lot may happen to be cast. For those who write books, those whose example extends beyond their own circle, the world is their parish. It is very difficult for anyone to calculate how far, how very far, even in this almost illimitable country, the effect of his influence may extend.

The world of America is, in a certain sense, the parish of everyone who hears me. On the effect of the examples which you, young or old, layman or pastor, may hold forth, the destinies of this country to a great degree may hang. It is so in all lands. It must be especially so in a country like this, where public opinion, where the opinion of the people at large, is supposed to have so great a sway. Do not for a moment suppose that you can wink at individual corruption and yet leave the world of this great country uninjured. Each one of you must remember that whether in giving your votes, or in writing for newspapers, or in whatever sphere you may be exercising any influence at all, that influence may reach far beyond the parish or place in which your daily duties lie—"the world is your parish."

Another point on which Wesley laid stress was the principle that it was not desirable to have preachers and teachers and pastors stationed in one place, but that the standard of religion and morality had to be constantly quickened and freshened by the system of itinerant preachers and pastors, who were to enliven and revive religious feeling from time to time, from season to season, in places where otherwise decay and dulness might have set in. You will, here too, allow me to say that the opposite principle has also some value. There is some value in a pastor growing up amongst his people, a pastor who has seen successive generations growing up around him—when to the influence of his preaching is added the far greater and more spiritual influence of a long life of good example, known and loved by the fathers and children of all the homes that are gathered within reach of the parish church. Yet we ought all to feel that there is, nevertheless, such a thing as the necessity of enlightening and refreshing these more stationary pastorates by the introduction of new influences, new hopes, new instruments, such as John Wesley had in mind when he conceived his design of itinerant preachers. In the old country this has been to a large extent acknowledged by the introduction of special services and sermons over and above the stated and regular ministrations. To a certain degree the Church of England has profited by his warnings; and the services and sermons which have now been set on foot in almost every cathedral of England—varying the stationary teaching by the constant introduction of new preachers, coming again and again, so as to infuse new life into these old congregations and a new spirit into these old grooves—are examples of the manner in which John Wesley's principles may be engrafted into Churches seeming at first to be very far removed from Wesleyan institutions.

There is yet one further remark which I would venture to make on the character and career of John Wesley. Everyone who knows anything of his long and eventful course will know that there are many points in it which it is difficult to defend or to reconcile. But the question always arises in any person of historical magnitude—such a man as your famous founder—what was the primary, fundamental, overruling principle of his whole character and teaching? And for this we have the best possible testimonies. We have the testimony—I have heard it myself—from humble Methodists in England, aged persons who had hung upon his lips and seen him in the cottages of the poor. We have also the testimony —I know not whether you are acquainted with it, but if not I strongly recommend it to the study and perusal of every Methodist, whether in England or America—we have the testimony of a most enlightened and distinguished layman, who was his intimate friend, and who judged him not merely like his more enthusiastic and unlettered followers, but with the full discernment of character which superior intelligence and refined religion alone can give. I mean Alexander Knox.

He has described him to us in terms most striking and persuasive, in the letter appended to the latest edition of Southey's "Life of Wesley." He has recorded his conviction that the main fundamental overpowering principle of Wesley's life was not the promotion of any particular dogma or any particular doctrine, but the elevation of the whole Christian world in the great principles of Christian holiness and morality. I might enforce this by many extracts from this letter of Mr. Knox, or by expressions both of his humble and of his more intelligent followers; but it is enough to refer you to the sayings and sermons in which this principle is again and again repeated with every kind of emphasis by John Wesley himself. You will see it in his journals, you will see it in his sermons on the catholic spirit, and on the Beatitudes, those admirable sermons to which all Methodists express their adhesion. There is one passage, which I have selected out of hundreds, which I trust you will allow me to read to you, both because it gives in the most emphatic and attractive language this principle of his mission, and also because it expresses that friendly and kindly relation which, as in the former part of this address, I endeavoured to show to you, existed between him and the high authorities of the Church of England. Let me give one single extract: "Near fifty years ago, a great and good man, Dr. Potter, then Archbishop of Canterbury, gave me an advice for which I have ever since had occasion to bless God. 'If you desire to be extensively useful, do not spend your time and strength in contending for or against such things as are of a disputable nature, but in testifying against open notorious vice, and in promoting real essential holiness.' Let us keep to this, leaving a thousand disputable points to those that have no better business than to toss the ball of controversy to and fro; let us keep close to our point; let us bear a faithful testimony, in our several stations, against all ungodliness and unrighteousness, and, with all our might, recommend that inward and outward holiness, 'without which no man shall see the Lord.'"

It is this which endears the memory of John Wesley, not only to his own society, not only to the Church of England, but to all who wish for the welfare and the progress of humanity throughout the whole world.

It is because of the keenness and the pertinacity with which John Wesley maintained this fundamental doctrine of Christianity that I rejoice to think that he is honoured amongst the kings and heroes, amongst the great, whether in literature or science, whose monuments adorn the walls of Westminster Abbey.

I thank you all, bishops and pastors, who sit around me. I thank you also, members of the Methodist Episcopal Church, by whom this building is so densely filled. I thank you all for the generous and unexpected sympathy, with which I have been received among you in this my too brief visit to this great country and to this famous city.

VII.

REPLY

AT THE BREAKFAST GIVEN BY THE CENTURY CLUB, NEW YORK,
NOVEMBER 2, 1878.

THE hospitality shown to me has been no exception to that with which every Englishman meets in this country, in the endless repetition of kind words and the overwhelming pressure of genial entertainment which has been thrust upon me. That famous Englishman, Dr. Johnson, when he went from England to Scotland, which, at that time, was a more formidable undertaking than is a voyage from England to America at the present time, met at a reception at St. Andrew's a young professor who said, breaking the gloomy silence of the occasion: "I trust you have not been disappointed!" And the famous Englishman replied: "No; I was told that I should find men of rude manners and savage tastes, and I have not been disappointed." So, too, when I set out for your shores I was told that I should meet a kindly welcome and the most friendly hospitality. I can only say, with Dr. Johnson, I have not been disappointed.

But in my vivid though short experience of American life and manners, I have experienced not only hospitality, but considerate and thoughtful kindness, for which I must ever be grateful. I can find it in my heart even to forgive the reporters who have left little of what I have said or done unnoted, and when they have failed in this, have invented fabulous histories of things which I never did and sayings which I never uttered. Sometimes when I have been questioned as to my impressions and views of America, I have been tempted to say with an Englishman who was hard pressed by his constituents with absurd solicitations: "Gentlemen, this is the humblest moment of my life, that you should take me for such a fool as to answer all your questions." But I know their good intentions and I forgive them freely.

The two months which I have spent on these shores seem to me two years in actual work, or two centuries rather, for in them I have lived through all American history. In Virginia I saw the era of the earliest settlers, and I met John Smith and

Pocahontas on the shores of the James river. In Philadelphia I have lived with William Penn, but in a splendour, which I fear would have shocked his simple soul. At Salem I have encountered the stern founders of Massachussetts; at Plymouth I have watched the *Mayflower* threading its way round the shoals and promontories of that intricate bay. On Lake George and at Quebec I have followed the struggle between the English and the French for the possession of this great continent. At Boston and Concord I have followed the progress of the War of Independence. At Mount Vernon I have enjoyed the felicity of companionship with Washington and his associates. I pause at this great name, and carry my recollections no further. But you will understand how long and fruitful an experience has thus been added to my life, during the few weeks in which I have moved amongst the scenes of your eventful history.

And then leaving the past for the present, a new field opens before me. There are two impressions which are fixed upon my mind as to the leading characteristics of the people among whom I have passed, as the almanack informs me, but two short months. On the one hand I see that everything seems to be fermenting and growing, changing, perplexed, bewildering. In that memorable hour—memorable in the life of every man, memorable as when he sees the first view of the Pyramids, or of the snow-clad range of the Alps—in the hour when for the first time I stood before the cataracts of Niagara, I seemed to see a vision of the fears and hopes of America. It was midnight, the moon was full, and I saw from the suspension bridge the ceaseless contortion, confusion, whirl, and chaos, which burst forth in clouds of foam from that immense central chasm which divides the American from the British dominion; and as I looked on that ever-changing movement, and listened to that everlasting roar, I saw an emblem of the devouring activity, and ceaseless, restless, beating whirlpool of existence in the United States. But into the moonlight sky there rose a cloud of spray twice as high as the Falls themselves, silent, majestic, immovable. In that silver column, glittering in the moonlight, I saw an image of the future of American destiny, of the pillar of light which should emerge from the distractions of the present—a likeness of the buoyancy and hopefulness which characterises you both as individuals and as a nation.

You may remember Wordsworth's fine lines on

"Yarrow Unvisited, Visited, and Revisited." "America unvisited"—that is now for me a vision of the past; that fabulous America, in which, before they come to your shores, Englishmen believe Pennsylvania to be the capital of Massachusetts, and Chicago to be a few miles from New York—that has now passed away from my mind for ever. "America visited;" this, with its historic scenes and its endless suggestions of thought, has taken the place of that fictitious region. Whether there will ever be an "America revisited" I cannot say; but if there should be, it will then be to me not the land of the Pilgrim Fathers and of Washington, so much as the land of kindly homes, and enduring friendships, and happy recollections, which have now endeared it to me. One feature of this visit I fear I cannot hope to see repeated, yet one without which it could never have been accomplished. My two friends, to whom such a pleasing reference has been made by Dr. Adams, who have made the task easy for me which else would have been impossible; who have lightened every anxiety; who have watched over me with such vigilant care, that I have not been allowed to touch more than two dollars in the whole course of my journey—they, perchance, may not share in "America revisited." But if ever such should be my own good fortune, I shall remember it as the land which I visited with them; where, if at first they were welcomed to your homes for my sake, I have often felt as the days rolled on that I was welcomed for their sake. And you will remember them. When in after years you read at the end of some elaborate essay on the history of music or on Biblical geography the name of George Grove, you will recall with pleasure the incessant questionings, the eager desire for knowledge, the wide and varied capacity for all manner of instruction, which you experienced in your conversations with him here. And when also hereafter there shall reach to your shores the fame of the distinguished physician, Dr. Harper, whether in England or in New Zealand, you will be the more rejoiced because it will bring before you the memory of the youthful and blooming student who inspected your hospitals with such keen appreciation, so impartially sifting the good from the evil.

I part from you with the conviction that such bonds of kindly intercourse will cement the union between the two countries even more than the wonderful cable, on which it is popularly believed in England that my friend and host, Mr. Cyrus Field, passes his mysterious existence, appearing and reappearing at one and the same moment in London and in New York. Of that unbroken union there seemed to me a likeness, when on the beautiful shores of Lake George, the Loch Katrine of America, I saw a maple and an oak tree growing together from the same stem, perhaps from the same root—the brilliant fiery maple, the emblem of America; the gnarled and twisted oak, the emblem of England. So may the two nations always rise together, so different each from each, and representing so distinct a future, yet each springing from the same ancestral root, each bound together by the same healthful sap, and the same vigorous growth.

VIII.

REPLY

TO AN ADDRESS PRESENTED BY THE BAPTIST MINISTERS OF NEW YORK AND BROOKLYN, ON NOVEMBER 4, 1878.

PERHAPS you expect me to say a few words—but they must be I fear brief—in grateful acknowledgment for the kind reception which I have met in this city, and for the sentiments in the address which has just been read. It is certainly not too much for me to say that I regard the great Baptist denomination with deep interest.

I regard it with interest, first, because of the work which its pastors have done in America and England—but more particularly in America—towards the extension of religion among classes that we in our Church might find it difficult to reach. The Churches in this country and in England, as I have before remarked in one of my sermons, ought to be all fellow-labourers in the Christian work, each one doing that work for which it is peculiarly fitted. So it is that we ought to feel grateful to the Baptist Churches for aiding in a task which we ourselves could not accomplish. This is the first ground on which I would express my obligation to you.

Secondly, you have alluded to me, in your address, as an ecclesiastical historian, and have referred to the undoubted antiquity of your principal ceremony—that of immersion. I feel that here also we ought to be grateful to you for having, almost alone in the Western Church, preserved intact this singular and interesting relic of primitive and apostolic times, which we—you will forgive me for saying so—which we, at least in our practice, have wisely discarded.

To the third ground of my interest in the Baptist Church you have also alluded in your address. There can be no doubt that you have produced some Christians of such eminence and worth that they are reckoned amongst the wealth of all Christendom. Bunyan the writer, Robert Hall the preacher, Havelock the soldier, these are the men to the purity of whose lives, and to the strength of whose minds, we all owe so much. It is indeed difficult to learn from the

"Pilgrim's Progress" whether Bunyan was a Baptist or Pædobaptist, a Churchman or a Nonconformist; but this is the very reason why he is so important, because it shows that he belonged to that high order of genius which transcends all the limits that divide us into different denominations. Again, in the finest and most famous sermons of Robert Hall, which, unfortunately, I am not old enough to have heard myself, there was nothing in them by which you could ascertain whether he did or did not attach any value to immersion in baptism—yet we feel as we read those sermons that there was something in that magnificent eloquence, something in that dignified presentation of the Christian faith, which brought him into contact not only with your own body but with ours, and with all who have the heart and mind to understand one so highly gifted. Of Havelock I will only say what was told to me by a friend of mine, who spoke to his wife, and asked whether she knew how he bore himself during the terrible conflicts in India. His wife answered: "I have not heard from him for some time; but I am sure that, now as always, he is trusting in God and doing his duty." I know not whether Havelock in those moments looked back with most affection to our Church which he had left, or to yours which he had joined. But this answer is one in which we might all sympathise. "Trusting in God and doing our duty"—these are words which bind us all together. If you or I can feel that those who know us best can say of us that we are trusting in God and doing our duty, it is enough to teach us that this is a ground of communion which neither the difference of external rites, nor the difference of seas or continents, can ever efface.

IX.

THE PROSPECTS OF THE CHURCH OF ENGLAND.

SPOKEN AT A RECEPTION GIVEN BY THE CLERGY OF THE PROTESTANT EPISCOPAL CHURCH, IN NEW YORK, NOV. 4, 1878.

INVITED, as I am, by the remarks which have just been made, to say something on the prospects of the Church of England in relation to the progress of Liberal Theology, I will first offer a few observations on its external fortunes. Those who have preceded me have, I think rightly, spoken of Westminster Abbey as a typical likeness of these relations. So long as any Church or communion is placed by the State in possession of a national building like Westminster Abbey, so long there will be an Established Church in England. Those who wish for the destruction of the National Church must, by a logical process (as they have in fact announced in the programme of their intended scheme put forth to the world), sever all connection between that or other like national buildings and the offices of religion. The Abbey might, in that case, continue as a venerable monument, like the Round Towers of Ireland or the mounds in the American wilderness, but it would cease to be filled with that glow of historical and religious life which through its long history has distinguished it from a mere Walhalla or Museum. And, on the other hand, the secular and national influences which Westminster Abbey represents have an important bearing on the growth and spread of those liberal opinions in theology which are held by those who, here or elsewhere, express their sympathy with myself as their spokesman. But for the connection of the Church of England with the State, I myself should certainly never have been Dean of Westminster; and the comprehensive and large associations which the institution fosters and inspires have been an immense support to any individual convictions and utterances of my own, which find in those associations so ready and so vast an echo.

When I speak of my connection with the Liberal section of the Church of England, you will not wish or expect that I should consider myself here as representing that section only. It is the very characteristic of the Church of England that anyone who professes to express its more liberal aspirations cannot fail to claim kinship with all the varying shades of opinion which make up the whole institution, and which, by their close contact within the same Church, tend to enlarge and correct each separate tendency, including the tendency of Liberal Theology itself. It has been a source of deep gratification to me to find that the Protestant Episcopal Church of America, in the welcome which it has afforded to me, has understood this position, and has thereby proved the genuineness of its descent from the Mother Church. It has been almost beyond my expectations that I should have received such expressions of sympathy, not merely from those whom I knew to be in agreement with me, but from those who, on the right hand and on the left, might well have held aloof. To all such expressions I have felt myself bound to respond, not merely from a grateful sense of the kindness which they manifested, but from the conviction that I was thus best acting in conformity with the principles which I have always cherished and maintained. It has been a frequent saying of Mr. John Bright—not an unkindly neighbour of the Church of England—

that, if the Church were united within itself, it would stand for ever. On this I have often remarked, that if it were in absolute and uniform agreement through all its parts, its downfall would be already sealed. I am glad to recognise this same diversity in the Episcopal Church of America, and I trust that here, as in England, liberal Churchmen may be of service in protecting its more extreme sections from each other. And yet I feel that the American Episcopal Church ought to be, in a special sense, the natural home of the broader sentiments entertained by those whom I especially address. The characteristic changes which that Church introduced into its liturgy when, after the War of Independence, it became a separate body, were directly derived from the larger and more generous elements which animated the Church of England at the beginning of the last century. That attempt at enlightenment and conciliation, which was inspired by Tillotson, in the Jerusalem Chamber of Westminster, and which, unfortunately, failed with us through the madness of a clerical faction, was carried out here; and Tillotson, we all know, was the most statesmanlike and large-minded primate who has occupied the See of Canterbury till the present time, when his place is worthily filled by one whom the American bishops and clergy have learned to respect and to honour as we do, and who is specially endeared to them by the intimate knowledge which circumstances have given to them of that deep and overwhelming affliction with which it has pleased God recently to visit him. Those changes to which I have referred in the American Prayer-book, with hardly more than one exception, all run in the same upward direction; and however much the American Episcopal Church may, from time to time, have been led astray by influences similar to those which have retarded the progress of the Church of England, yet surely it is not too much to hope that the force of that original impulse and impact still continues, and will guide you safely onwards to the haven where you should be.

It is not for me to speak in detail of the relation of the Episcopal clergy of America to those of the other communions by which they are surrounded and in a certain sense overshadowed. Yet I have been rejoiced to observe so many indications on both sides of the disappearance of ancient barriers and the formation of new bonds of union. There is a passage in the Book of Genesis, on which I have often been accustomed to dwell, as a likeness of the course which we may hope that ecclesiastical history may take.

When Isaac digged a well in the valley of Gerar, the neighbouring herdsmen strove with him, and he called the name of that well *Esek*, that is to say, "strife or controversy;" and they went on to another well, and there also there were accusations and counter accusations, and he called the name of that well *Sitnah*, that is to say, "calumny," or "recrimination." And they went on and found another well in a large free open space, where each had room to feed their flocks at will, without interfering with the others, and he called the name of that well *Rehoboth*, that is to say, as it is in our version, "room," or "width" or "breadth," or as it is called in the sacred Vulgate of the ancient Church, *Latitudo*, or in plain English, "latitude." Latitude, or latitudinarian, is not deemed a reproach by that venerable translation; it was deemed the highest title of honour by the noblest English divines at the close of the seventeenth century. It may perchance be our best guide, even in the New World, to the still waters of comfort and peace.

One remark in conclusion. I have been asked whether, on some former occasions of addressing the clergy of this country, I have not spoken of the future in too desponding a tone. It is true that at times I feel that in this close of the nineteenth century we may be passing through a temporary eclipse. But there is only one permanent danger which I seem to discern as affecting all Churches alike. Let me illustrate it by a story from another scene. When, in a banquet given to him by the chief statesmen of Italy, Mr. Gladstone addressed them in a powerful speech on the glories of their country, in that beautiful Italian tongue of which he is so complete a master, he suddenly exclaimed: "But there is an enemy in the midst of you." They started; they turned to each other; they whispered: "He means the Pope." But for once Mr. Gladstone was not running on ecclesiastical controversies. He was thinking of an enemy in the heart of the Italian kingdom, familiar to the mundane experiences in which his transcendent financial powers made him more completely at home. He said: "His name is *Deficit*." May I apply this saying, not to the deficiency of revenues or receipts of which he spoke, but to the deficiency of young men of promise and power entering the ranks of the Christian ministry, whether in our Church or yours, or any of the other numerous Churches of either world. I know not how far you are menaced by this danger, but if you are, or if there be any apprehension on that score, I entreat you to be constantly on your watch to meet it, to lose no opportunity of removing any stumbling-block or obstacle which may deter such men from entering your ranks. If you, if we, can thus be kept on a level with the energy, the science, the nobleness, and the genius of the times in which we live, however dark may be the passing cloud, there will be no fear either for Liberal Theology or for the Christian Church in the age which is yet to come.

I part from you with these, as I believe, my last public utterances in America. The welcome which you have given to me I trust I may have the opportunity of repaying, when those of you who come to visit Westminster Abbey once more seek there the greeting which in former times was never absent, but which will now, as far as change of circumstances permit, be redoubled by the grateful recollection of the hospitality and the friendship which have met me here.

SERMONS.

PREFACE

TO THE FOLLOWING SERMONS.

ON THE CONDITIONS OF RELIGIOUS INQUIRY.

THE story of Jacob wrestling with the angel is one which, however we may interpret its literal meaning, undoubtedly lends itself in the original, even more than in our translation, to a deeper and more spiritual sense. The vision took place, we are told, in the crisis of Jacob's life. He was returning from Mesopotamia. He was on the eve of the meeting with his brother. Every incident, almost every word, is charged with a double meaning. There are the banks of the Jabbok, the "wrestling-stream" (such is the meaning of the word), wrestling, forcing its way through the rocky basins of the deep defile which parted the brothers asunder. There are the earthly "messengers" on whose intercession he relies; there are the heavenly "messengers" who are ranged behind them; there are the two "bands" or companies of his own tribe, and compared with them are the two "bands" or companies of angels. There is the "face" of his brother Esau, whom he longs but fears to see; there is the "face" of God, which also he fears yet longs to see. It is in the midst of these conflicting images, as in a dream, that he encounters he knows not whom on the mountainside. The wrestling of the torrent, with its tangled thickets and its rocky boundaries, bears a likeness to a yet mightier wrestling of the human soul with its deep perplexities and sorrows. Through the long watches of the night, the Patriarch is locked in a struggle as for life and death with the mysterious combatant, and he entreats that he may know his name. But when at last the dawn "rises" (so it is expressed in the original) over the hills of Gilead, he feels that his whole being is transfigured. "He said: 'I have seen God face to face, and my life is preserved.' And he called the name of the place Peniel, 'The Face of God.'" At that moment the twilight of the dawn "bursts" into full sunlight, and he summons courage to descend from the face of the mountain height, and plunges down into the narrow glen, and passes the fatal stream, and prepares himself for the dreaded interview. Always (such was the belief of his descendants) he bore with him the marks of that mighty conflict, "for he halted on his thigh." It was as though the agony of the conflict had dislocated even his earthly frame. Henceforth "few and evil were the days of his pilgrimage." Nor do we ever lose entirely the recollection of the wily son of Rebekah. But still the grander, nobler part prevailed; the dark crafty Jacob, the treacherous supplanter of his brother Esau, disappeared and became "Israel," the Prince of God, the Conqueror of God, the founder of the mighty nation which still bears his glorious name. On that day, as it were, in the depths of his spiritual being were born Moses and David, Elijah and Isaiah, and One greater than all, who was indeed the Prince of God, and should prevail for ever.

This encounter, as I have said, has been considered as the likeness, almost without an allegory, of all spiritual struggles. It is the groundwork of one of the finest hymns in our language — that in which Charles Wesley describes the appeal of the struggling human soul to the mysterious Stranger whom it meets on its passage through life:

> Come, O thou traveller unknown,
>   Whom still I hold, but cannot see.
> My company before is gone,
>   And I am left alone with Thee.
> With Thee all night I mean to stay
> And wrestle till the break of day.

It has been made the groundwork of an interesting discourse by the greatest English preacher of this century, Frederick Robertson. It was the constant burden of a gifted Bishop of the Scottish Episcopal Church, who, if any one of our day, wrestled with the questions of his time till his fragile frame was broken by the force of the spiritual conflict.

There are indeed numberless experiences of individual existence which the story represents to us. It describes the struggles which every autobiography reveals—the entrance on a new stage of life, the decision on a profession, the inrush of new thoughts, the wrestle with temptations, with circumstances, with sorrows. It represents how the common things of life are to us the indications of the Divine presence. The "bands" of our friends and companions become to us "bands" of ministering spirits. In the chime of familiar bells we hear a voice bidding us turn again and take heart. In reading the pathetic scene of another's early trials, John Stuart Mill finds the dried-up fountains of his heart unlocked, and after years of premature hardness is born again as a little child. In the whispering of the mountain torrent, as we find ourselves in some long forgotten, but instantly remembered, scene of former years—

> All along the valley, down its rocky bed
> The living voice to us is as the voice of the dead.

It describes also the last struggle of all, it may be in the extreme of age or of weakness, in the valley of the shadow of death. There the soul finds itself alone on the mountain ridge overlooking the unknown future; "our company before is gone," the kinsfolk and friends of many years are passed over the dark river, and we are left alone with God. We know not in the shadow of the night who it is that touches us—we feel only that the Everlasting Arms are closing us in; the twilight of the morning breaks, we are bid to depart in peace, for by a strength not our own we have prevailed, and the path is made clear before us.

There is also another struggle—another wrestling—that which takes place between the human spirit and the vast mysterious problems by which we are surrounded. In every age this struggle takes place, in some perhaps more than in others, and it may be that such an age is ours. "Such questioning," it has been wisely said, "necessarily belongs to every transition state,* a transition which every age and every soul must make from an unintelligent assent to a traditional creed towards an intelligent assent to a true faith :" not all light nor all darkness, but still, as we humbly trust, from darkness into light.

To many, all such mental struggles will be unknown and unsought. There was no wrestling with God in the early patriarchal days of Abraham and Isaac. Let those, if such there be, who live in that old ancestral peace continue so to live; only let them not pretend to wrestle when they are in no difficulty. It is very rarely indeed that the sudden changes from church to church, or the adoption of this or that strange practice or form, are the results of deliberate doubt or search. They are more commonly the mere change of one fancy for another, or a leap from darkness into darkness. It is not

---

* "Reflections and Reminiscences of John M'Leod Campbell," p. 256.

of these that we would speak. But for those who are exercised on the great problems of Religion and Theology, it may be not presumptuous to suggest four homely maxims, impressed upon us alike by the Bible and by human experience.

(1.) Any such conflict, whether of mind or spirit, must be serious and in earnest. It must be an anxious endeavour to gain that which we seek. "I will not let thee go except thou bless me." The expression is bold even to the verge of irreverence. But it is not irreverence, because nothing is more reverent than an earnest determination of purpose. It is not playfulness or gaiety of heart that we deprecate—in God's name, keep of that as much as can possibly be had. It is not that which makes a soul unstable or hollow. But asking questions without waiting for an answer; talking merely for the sake of victory; treating sacred and important questions as party flags, to be hoisted up or pulled down, according as it suits the ebb and flow of public opinion—all this is no struggle, no inquiry at all. This is levity, this is foolish jesting—mere vanity and vexation of spirit. Whoever repeats the phrases of religion or of irreligion, merely to astonish or bewilder, or to conceal his ignorance, or to gain momentary popularity; whoever enters on the questions of religious thought without a determined intention of doing or saying what is best for his own conscience and for the consciences of others, is a profane person, by whatever name he calls himself. But a man who is possessed with what the French call "the grand curiosity" of knowing all that can be known, he who looks up to the truly great authorities of all ages and countries, to the high intelligences of unquestioned fame and worth that God has raised up to enlighten the world—he has made an effort to enter on the narrow path, and to force his way through the strait gate that leads to eternal life. The very struggle to him is good. The very awe of these great questions produces in his mind the reverence which is the first element of religion. That was a true name which the old Greeks employed to describe a good man, a religious man. They called him "a man of business"—a man in earnest, a man who felt the gravity of what he was doing and saying. Such a man, no doubt, may get his conscience warped, or may become fanatical or self-deceived; but so far as his seriousness goes, he is right; so far as his seriousness is sincere, whatever be his errors, he is on the right way, and God is not far from him. Not what others think for us, but what we are able to think for ourselves is the true life of our life. Well said the German poet: "The secret of Genius is first, next, and without end to honour truth *by use.*" Struggle, wrestle with the meaning of the sacred words which we employ. Take them not in vain. Where we cannot find their meaning they are to us as though they were not; we had best not apply them at all. But in all those that are worth retaining—as in all the dispensations of life and nature—there is what in the story of Jacob is called a "Face," an aspect, of God which looks out at us from behind the darkness if we gaze steadily in the right direction.

(2.) Every such inquiry must be carried on with the conviction that truth only is to be sought. As perfect love casts out fear, so perfect confidence in truth casts out fear. That old proverb of the Apocryphal Book of Esdras is not the less excellent because it is so familiar: "Great is the truth, and stronger than all things." "Magna est veritas et prævalebit." * Jacob is described as struggling, wrestling with the unknown

---

* 1 *Esdras* iv. 35. The words of the original text are: "Magna est veritas et *prævalet.*" The change from the present tense, *prævalet,* "is strong," to the future, *prævalebit,* "will be strong," indicates the increasing conviction in Christendom of the ultimate victory of Truth.

mystery. He knew not what to make of it, but it prevailed at last over him and he prevailed with it. It is the very likeness of the search of a sincere soul after Truth. Often the Truth may elude our search, may slip from our grasp, may fling us on the ground; but if we cling fast to it, some portion of it will be ours at last, and we in its triumph shall be more than conquerors. A venerable divine of the Roman Church has,* in our time, powerfully described the human intellect under the figure of a ravenous wild beast that has to be driven back by the iron bar of authority, "smiting hard and throwing back the immense energy of the aggressive intellect," lest it should, as it were, devour and dissolve all things, Divine and human, in its insatiable appetite. This is surely not the figure presented to us in Jacob's vision or in the Bible generally. The Truth that is really Divine does not smite down its combatant. Nay, rather it allows itself to be embraced, repulsed, embraced again, seized now by this side, now by that, lifted up, pressed, challenged to surrender. "Come, let us reason together." "The Lord will plead with Israel." "We can do nothing against the Truth, but for the Truth."

* Dr. Newman's "Apologia," pp. 381, 382.

The human intellect has had placed before it by Him who made it, one object and one only, worthy of its efforts, and that is Truth—Truth, not for the sake of any ulterior object, however high or holy, but Truth for its own sake. We hope, we trust, we humbly believe, that Truth will in the end be found to coincide with goodness, with holiness, with grace, with humility, with all the other noblest aspirations of the human spirit. But if we think and reason on these high matters at all, we must seek and desire Truth even as though it existed by and for itself alone. And the most excellent service that Churches and pastors, authorities of State or of Religion, universities or teachers, can render to the human reason in this arduous enterprise is not to restrain, nor to blindfold it, but to clear aside every obstacle, to open wide the path, to chase away the phantoms that stand in the road. Above all, it is alike the high calling of true philosophy and Christian civilisation, to rise beyond the reach of the blinding, bewildering, entangling influence of the spirit of party. It was once said by Archbishop Whately that the chief evil of the modern Church of Rome was not transubstantiation, or the worship of the saints, or purgatory, or any other of the special opinions held by its members, but the fact that it was "a great party," inspired by the same motives and guided by the same principles as bind together sects and parties, political or other, throughout the world. So far as the Church of Rome or any other Church is not this, even its errors are comparatively innocent; so far as it is this, its very truths become mischievous. "Whatever retards a spirit of inquiry," said Robert Hall, "is favourable to error. Whatever promotes it, is favourable to truth. But nothing has greater tendency to obstruct the exercise of free inquiry than a spirit of party. There is in all sects and parties a constant fear of being eclipsed. It becomes a point of honour with the leaders of parties to defend and support their respective peculiarities to the last, and, as a natural sequence, to shut their ears against all the pleas by which they may be assailed. If we seek for the reason of the facility with which scientific improvements establish themselves in preference to religious, we shall find it in the absence of party combination." No doubt even the domain of science has not been free from the passions and personalities of party teachers; but the great Nonconformist whom I have just cited had good ground—had, I may almost say, Divine authority—for directing his special warning to the religious world. This spirit of combination for party purposes, and this alone, is what the New Testament calls "heresy." This it is that constitutes the leading danger of synods and councils, which, by their very constitution, become almost inevitably the organs, never of full and impartial truth, almost always of misleading ambiguities which tend rather to darkness than to light, rather to confusion than to union.

(3.) We must in our inquiry be on the watch as far as we can, not for something to attack, but for something to admire; not for something to pull down, but for something to build up. "Prove all things," says the Apostle, and he almost immediately afterwards adds, "abstain from every kind* of evil," that is, from every kind of evil, however specious, however religious may be its appearance. This, no doubt, is an important maxim. The negative side of Christianity, - the formation of an atmosphere in which whole classes of falsehood have been unable to live, is a merit which has been hardly enough appreciated. But the more direct maxim of the Apostle is still more important: "Prove all things; *hold fast that which is good.*" It has been too often the conventional strategy of theological argument, in dealing with books or persons with whom

---

* 1 *Thess.* v. 21, 22 (in the original).

we differ, to give no quarter; to treat them as wizards were treated down to the middle of the seventeenth century, as though they were embodied and absolute evil—as if the moment we find ourself face to face with such a book or such a line of argument, the first thing to be done is to tear it to pieces, and pick out all its worst parts, and take for granted the worst possible construction. Far be it from us to deny that there are books so worthless, characters and principles so detestable, that they demand all the indignation of which the human soul is capable. But these are exceptions. Far oftener, when we are perplexed and distressed, the impression is as of the vision in the Book of Job: "Fear cometh upon me and trembling; a spirit passed before me, but I could not discern the form thereof; the image was before mine eyes, and there was silence." In the larger part of such books as from their fame and weight demand to be read, as there are none which are uniformly good, so there are very few which are uniformly evil. In all we must discriminate. Even the Bible itself has its gradations. The Old Testament, great as it is, is not so Divine as the New. The Apocalypse, splendid as are its imagery and its purpose, is not so edifying as the Gospels or the Psalms. It was said of the Koran that it had two faces, one of a beast, to scandalise the weak, one of a seraph, to attract the faithful. That, to a certain extent, is the case even in the Bible; it is the case certainly with all other good books. There is the face of the beast which may terrify; but there is the face of the seraph to delight us, and he is the best inquirer who, while he acknowledges the face of the beast, yet turns away from it to gaze chiefly on the face of the seraph. We are justly indignant with ignorant or foolish scoffers, who in speaking of the Bible speak only of its obscure, harsh, and perplexing passages; who omit the Sermon on the Mount, and speak only of the questionable acts of the Patriarchs; who omit the glory of the hundred and nineteenth Psalm, and dwell only on the curses of the hundred and ninth; who speak only of the rare anathemas and pass over the long-suffering love, of the Parables in the Gospels or of the Epistles of St. Paul. But we should be no less indignant with ourselves or with others, if, in speaking or reading of books of science, books of philosophy, books of religion, we look at them only to extract the evil, the controversial, the offensive, the frivolous; and overlook the genius, the wisdom, the knowledge, the goodness, which, whilst disagreeing ever so much, we might yet discover in them for our eternal benefit. It is astonishing how vast a loss we sustain for our spiritual life by thinking only how we can destroy, attack, and assail, instead of thinking how we can build up, define, or edify. There is not a book in the world, however great or good, which would stand the test of being taken only in its weaker points. There are very few books of any name or fame in the world which will not confirm our faith or raise our minds, if judged, not by passion or prejudice, but on their own merits, "according to righteous judgment." Jacob wrestled to the end through darkness and light, and in the end he felt that his unknown enemy was no enemy at all, but the same vision of angels that he had seen at Bethel, the kind and merciful face of God, the God of his father Abraham, and of his father Isaac.

(4.) Yet one more rule. Let us enter on these inquiries, not in despair, but in hope. There is doubtless enough to discourage. Sometimes we think that we are about to be overwhelmed by a general return of forgotten superstitions, sometimes by a general chaos of incredulity; sometimes our course seems darkened by an eclipse of faith, sometimes by an eclipse of reason. Yet, on the whole, the history of mankind justifies us in hoping that as in the moral, so also in the intellectual condition of the race, in regard to these higher spiritual truths, our light is not altogether swallowed up in darkness, that the good cannot be and is not altogether lost, that the evil, the error, the superstition, that has once disappeared, even if it returns from time to time, will not again permanently rule over us as heretofore. Christianity itself goes through these struggles. In its Divine aspect it wrestles with man. In its human aspect it wrestles with God. It has within it, like the Patriarch, two natures—the crafty, earth-born Jacob, the lofty, heaven-aspiring Israel.

Only we must acknowledge, let us rather say we must insist on, two conditions, if we would draw hope from the experience of religious history. First, we must acknowledge the immense changes through which Christianity has passed. It is because there is hardly any one form of Christian truth which has been held "always, everywhere, and by everybody," that we seem to see how it may at last assimilate to itself all the good and all the truth which the world contains, and which, though not in it, are yet of it. So far as it has survived the conflicts of eighteen centuries, it has been not by adhering rigidly to the past, but by casting off its worser and grosser elements, and taking up in each age something of that higher element which each age had to give. It has survived the corruptions and superstitions which it inherited from the Roman Empire, and has carried off in the struggle the elements of Roman civilisation. It has survived the miserable controversies of the fourth, fifth, and sixth centuries, and has carried off from its earlier age the first germs of liturgical worship and the memory of the martyrs. It has survived the barbarous fancies and cruelties of the Middle Ages, and carried off with it the marvels of mediæval art. It has survived the fierce conflicts of the Reformation, and has carried off with it the light of freedom, of conscience, and of knowledge. It has survived the shock of the French Revolution, and has carried off with it the toleration and the justice of the eighteenth century. It has survived the alarms which were excited at the successive appearance of Astronomy, Geology, Physiology, Historical Criticism, and has carried off with it a deeper insight into nature and into the Bible. In each of these anxious wrestling matches it has, like the Patriarch, seen the Face of God, and its life has been not only preserved but transfigured. Jacob, the old, treacherous, exclusive Jacob, has with each of these receded; Israel, the princely, the venerable, the loving father of the chosen people, has gradually prevailed.

And there is the second condition, that we must look for the true face of our religion in the face of those who have best represented it. We sometimes claim, and justly claim, as the glory of our faith, that it has attracted to itself the strength of intellects such as Shakespeare and Newton, Pascal and Rousseau, Erasmus and Spinosa, Goethe and Walter Scott. But then do we sufficiently remember what is the aspect of Christianity which commanded the reverential attention of men so different each from each? Was it the Christianity of Nicæa, or Geneva, or Westminster, or Augsburg, or the Vatican? No. It was, by the very nature of the case, something of a far more delicate texture, of a far deeper root.

Again, we may find an indication of the permanent character of Christianity when we ask what is the form of it defended by its chief apologists. The Christianity for which Paley argued in his "Evidences," and Lardner in his "Credibilia," and Butler in his "Sermons" and "Analogy," and Pascal in his "Thoughts," and Channing in his "Discourses"—was this the Calvinist, or the Lutheran, or the Wesleyan, or the Tridentine, or the Racovian Creed? No; for to each one of those stout champions of the faith, one or other of those forms would have been as revolting as that which they advocated was precious to them.

Again, it is the religion which has inspired the course of states and nations. Read the concise but subtle account given of the influence of Christianity on civilisation by the present Dean of St. Paul's, or the more extended examination of it in the history of Latin Christianity by his famous predecessor—read either of these works, or watch, if we prefer it, the gradual development of Christian art, from the Good Shepherd of the Catacombs to the Transfiguration of Raphael, from the majestic basilica to the soaring lines of the Gothic cathedral. Whilst we acknowledge in them the triumphant progress of what is best in Christianity, shall we not also acknowledge that it is a progress to which the Councils, the Confessions, even the Fathers and Schoolmen, have contributed almost nothing, and the general spirit of the race and the faith almost everything?

And is not the religion which animated these higher intelligences and these wider spheres the same which has animated the poor, the humble, the child-like, the saintlike of all persuasions? We do not deny that at particular epochs of excitement, the temporary opinions of particular schools and times may have filled the soul with heavenly fervour, that the doctrines of the "Invention of the Cross," or "the Sacred Heart," or "the Immaculate Conception"—of "Imputed Righteousness," of "Sudden Conversion," of "Episcopal Succession," of "Non-intrusion," may have swayed whole assemblies of men with one common impulse, or lighted up the last moments of departing saints with celestial energy. But these have been the mere wreaths of foam on the waves of enthusiasm. The perpetual undercurrent of devotion has been of another sort. "Pray for me," said an eminent French pastor on his death-bed, "that I may have the elementary graces." Those elementary graces are to be found in the great moral principles which lie at the bottom of the barbarous phraseology in which the sentiments of the poor, living or dying, are often expressed. It was but recently* that there was recorded the saying of an old Scottish Methodist, who in his earlier years had clung vehemently to one or other of the two small sects on either side of the street: "The street I'm now travelling in, lad, has nae sides; and if power were given

---

* "Reminiscences of the Pen-Folk, by One who knew them," p. 41.

me, I would preach purity of life mair, and purity of doctrine less than I did." "Are you not a little heretical at your journey's end?" said his interlocutor. "I kenna. Names have not the same terror on me they once had, and since I was laid by here alone, I have had whisperings of the still small voice, telling me that the footfall of faiths and their wranglings will ne'er be heard in the Lord's kingdom whereunto I am nearing. And as love cements all differences, I'll perhaps find the place roomier than I thought in times by-past."

And finally, the converging testimony rendered by so many different experiences towards the triumph of a higher Christianity is crowned by the testimony of the Bible itself. That the theology of the Bible is something beside and beyond, something greater and vaster than the theology of each particular Church or age, is proved by the fact that on the one hand it has never been found sufficient for the purposes of tests and polemics, and, on the other hand, that whenever the different schools of theologians have been brought together on its platform, either for selecting extracts for the public services of the Church, or for revising its translations, the points of division have fallen aside, the points of union have come to light, and the points of discussion have for the most part had no bearing on the divisions or the theories of Christendom. It is in the various aspects of the theology of the Bible—which is also the theology of European literature—the theology of great men, the theology of the saints, and the theology of the poor and of little children, that we may hope to see the Face of God.

We complain of the unfairness of the German critic who attacked the possibility of a Christian faith by directing his artillery against the coarsest and grossest forms in which that faith has been supported by any of its adherents. But this should be a solemn warning to us to see how far we have ourselves identified it with those forms. We smile at the narrowness of the English philosopher who regarded Christianity as the completest development of human wickedness, because he fixed his mind on one particular doctrine sometimes preached in its name. But this should be a solemn warning to us, to see how far such a doctrine is one for which we ourselves have contended as essential to the faith. True Christianity is beyond the reach of such attacks or such defences. Those who have watched the effects of sunrise on the Alpine ranges will remember the dark and chill aspect of the wide landscape in the moment preceding the dawn. At last there arose at once in the western and the eastern heavens a colour, a brightness, a lightness—varying, diffused, indefinite, but still spreading and brightening and lightening, over the whole scene. Then, "as in a moment, in the twinkling of an eye," the highest summits of the range of snow burst from pale death into roseate life, and every slope and crest became as clear and bright as before they had been dark and dull; and meanwhile the same light was creeping round the mists of the plain and the exhalations of the lakes, and they too were touched by gold, and every shape and form yielded to the returning glow. Such is an image of the rise of true religion, and therefore also of true theology, shadowy, diffused, expansive as the dawn, yet like the dawn striking with irresistible force now here, now there, first on the highest intelligences, then on the world at large, till at length the whole atmosphere is suffused with its radiance, and the shades of night have melted we hardly know how or where.

Such is the process by which the great regenerating truths of religion have made their way, and still make their way into the heart of man—truths not the less religious because they have often come from seemingly opposite quarters, truths which gain their place the more certainly because they come not in a polemic, but a pacific garb, not conquering, but subduing; not attacking error, but creating a light in which the shadows insensibly flee away. "Falsehood can only be said to be killed when it is replaced." Truth vanquishes only when it can enlist the religious enthusiasm that is too often the heritage of error. Enthusiasm can only be fully commended when it is enlisted on behalf of the wider and nobler instincts of the good and wise throughout mankind.

When the struggle is drawing to its end, when the day breaks and the sun rises, there will have been some who in that struggle have seen the Face of God.

I.

THE EAST AND THE WEST.

PREACHED IN TRINITY CHURCH, BOSTON, SUNDAY MORNING, SEPTEMBER 22, 1878.

In the ninth verse of the hundred and thirty-ninth Psalm are these words: "If I take the wings of the morning, and dwell in the uttermost parts of the sea, even there shall Thy hand lead me, and Thy right hand shall hold me."

In this utterance of the Psalmist, as in the whole Psalm, the most simple meaning is the expression of belief in the omnipresent power of God. The traveller who passes from one quarter of the globe to another, feels that the encircling sky which girdles in the ocean is but a type of the unseen Power that surrounds us all. It is the same truth as that expressed in the last words of one of the earliest English navigators in American waters: "Heaven is as near to us on the sea as on the land." The philanthropist, whose wide charity embraces within its grasp the savage and the civilised man, the white man and the negro, feels that the hand of God is with him in his enterprises, because in the face of all his fellow-men he recognises, however faintly and feebly delineated, the image of the likeness of God. Howard and Wilberforce, Eliot and Channing, were alike sustained by the thought that, in the widest diversities of human nature, and in the lowest depths of human degradation, God was with their efforts, because in the better part of every human being there was a spark of the Divine spirit. The philosopher who endeavours to trace out the unity of mankind, and the unity of all created things, consciously or unconsciously expresses the same truth; namely, that our Maker's eye saw our substance yet being imperfect, and that "in His book were all our members written, which day by day were fashioned" and evolved, "while as yet there were none of them," while all was as yet rudimental and undeveloped, alike in the individual and in the race. The heart-stricken, lonely, doubting sufferer, who sees only a step before him, who can but pray, "Lead, kindly Light, amid the encircling gloom"—he too can echo the words of the Psalmist: "The darkness is no darkness to Thee; the darkness and light to Thee are both alike." "Though He slay me, yet will I trust in Him."

But in the especial form of the words of the text there is a peculiar force, which it is my purpose on this occasion to bring before you. The Psalmist wishes to indicate that God was to be found in those regions of the earth into which it was least likely that any Divine influence should penetrate; and he expresses it by saying: "If I were to take the wings of the morning, if I were to mount on the outspreading radiance which in the eastern heavens precedes the rise of dawn, if I were to follow the sun on his onward course, and pass with him over land and ocean till I reach the uttermost parts of the sea, far away in the distant and unknown 'West'"—for in the original the two words mean the same thing—"even there also, strange as it may seem, the hand of God will lead us, the right hand of God will hold us; even there also, beyond the shadows of the setting of the sun, even there, beyond the farthest horizon, the farthest West of the farthest sea, will be found the Presence which leaps over the most impassable barriers." To the Psalmist, living in Palestine, living in those regions which were then the sole seat, not only of religion, but of civilisation and knowledge also, this expression was the most forcible mode which he could adopt of saying that nowhere in the wide world could he wander from the care of the Almighty; and in so saying he has, whether intentionally or not, given utterance to a truth to which the other parts of the Bible bear witness, but which receives its full confirmation in the New Testament, and its full realisation in the history of Christendom and of the modern world. That which seemed to him so portentous as to be almost incredible, has become one of the familiar, we might almost say one of the fundamental, axioms of our religious and social existence. "Not only in the East"—so we may venture to give his words their fullest and widest meaning—"not only in the East, consecrated by patriarchal tradition and usage, but in the unknown and distant islands and seas of the West, the power of God shall be felt as a sustaining help and guiding hand."

True religion, the point of contact between the East and the West, this is the thought upon which I propose to dwell. And, first, let us observe the actual fact in human experience. The contrast between the East and West is one of the most vivid which strikes the mind of man. Of the great geo graphical impressions left even on the most casual observer, none is deeper than that which is produced when a child of Western civilisation sets foot on the shores of the Eastern world. And so in history, as has been observed by a profound student, two distinct streams of human interest have always followed the race of Shem and the race of Japhet; but the turning points, the critical moments of their history, have been when the two streams have crossed each other, and met, as on a few great occasions, in conflict or in union. It is the very image which is presented to us in the splendid vision of the Evangelical Prophet in the sixtieth chapter of the book of Isaiah. The seer lifts up his eyes, and beholds on one side all the nations of the East, with all the peculiarities of custom and of dress such as have endured from his time to ours — dromedaries and camels, golden ornaments from India, clouds of incense from Arabia, flocks and herds of the wandering tribes of Arabia and Tartary—all crowding to receive the blessings of the future. And this was fulfilled; for we are never allowed to forget that Christ was born of an Eastern nation, clothed in Eastern dress, speaking in an Eastern language, familiar with Eastern sky and land. He was of the seed of Abraham, the first wanderer from the Eastern hills; of Isaac, brother of the Arabian Ishmael; of David and Solomon, Oriental kings. To His Eastern birthplace the Churches of the West have ever turned with peculiar reverence, and his Eastern home and Eastern tomb have been the points around which the conflicts of Europe again and again, and even in our own recent time, have turned.

There is an interest, as of our childish days, with which we cannot but regard the cradle of our race and of our faith, an interest not the less keen because that early sunrise of mankind has now been left so very far behind. The wings of the morning may flag and fail, but not so the purpose of God. It extends to the noon and to the evening no less. We must not look eastward, we must not look backward, if we would know the true strength of human progress and of Christ's religion. Westward, far into the westward sea, the Prophet looked, when, after beholding the dromedaries and camels of Arabia coming from the East, he turned to that distant horizon, and exclaimed: "Who are these that fly as a cloud, and as the doves to their windows?" "The isles"—that is, the isles, and coasts, and promontories, and creeks, and bays of the Mediterranean and Atlantic shores—" the isles shall wait for him, and the ships of Tarshish first." Tarshish, that is, the West, with all its vessels of war and its vessels of merchandise; the ships of Tarshish first, of Phœnicia and Carthage and Spain —these first brought the shores of Cornwall, the name of Britain, within the range of the old civilised world. All these, with their energy and activity, were to build up the walls, and pour their wealth through the gates of the heavenly Jerusalem. And so in fact it has been. Westward went the Apostle of the Gentiles, when starting from the coast of Syria he embarked on what a great French writer has called the "Christian Odyssey;" westward to that island which alone emerged on the horizon of the Israelite as he looked from the heights of Lebanon, the spot which was to him the sole representative of the westward races, the isle of Chittim, the isle of Cyprus, destined, perchance, in our later day to give back to the Eastern races what it once received from them. Westward the Apostle still advanced when he crossed over from Asia into Europe, and came into contact with the civilisation of Greece; westward yet again when he reached the mighty capital of the Western dominion; westward farther still when he stretched his yearning gaze toward what was then called the last limit of the world, the Pillars of Hercules, the extreme border of Spain. And so it has been through the long history of Christendom. The Eastern Churches, in spite of all their manifold interest, have not been the true centres of Christianity. They may have their destiny and their mission; but it is in Italy, in France, in Germany, in England, in America, that the hopes of Christian civilisation rest. Christianity, born in the East, has become the religion of the West even more than the religion of the East. Only by travelling from its early home has it grown to its full stature. The more it has adapted itself to the wants of the new-born nations, which it embraces, the more has it resembled the first teaching and character of its Founder and of His followers. Judaism, as a supreme religion, expired when its local sanctuary was destroyed. Mohammedanism, after its first burst of conquest, withdrew almost entirely within the limits of the East. But Christianity has found not only its shelter and refuge, but its throne and sanctuary, in countries which, humanly speaking, it could hardly have been expected to reach at all. From these Western countries, in spite of their manifold imperfections, that Eastern religion still sways the destinies of mankind. Under the shadow of that tree which sprang up from a grain of mustard-seed on the hills of Galilee, have been gathered the nations of the earth. The Christian religion rose on the "wings of the morning," but it has remained in the "uttermost parts of the sea," because the hand of God was with it, and the right hand of God was upholding it.

And now let us briefly consider what were the peculiar points of Christianity which have enabled it to combine these two worlds of thought, each so different from the other. In its full development, in its earliest and most authentic representation, we see the completion of those gifts and graces which East and West possess separately, and which we each are bound in our measure to appropriate.

(1.) First observe, on the one hand, in the Gospel History, the awe, the reverence, the profound resignation to the Divine Will, the calm, untroubled repose, which are the very qualities possessed by the Eastern religions at a time when to the West they were almost wholly unknown, and which even now are more remarkably exhibited in Eastern nations than amongst ourselves. "Thy will be done," that great prayer which lies at the root of all religion, is a thought which the old Western nations hardly understood. It breathes the spirit of the race of Abraham, of the race of Ishmael. "God is great," so a Mussulman Algerine once said to his Christian captive. The captive, who came from the British Isles, has recorded that it was the first word of consolation that had reached his heart, and caused his sinking spirit to revive. On the other hand, look at the practical activity and beneficence which formed the sum and substance of the Redeemer's life; how He went about everywhere doing good, how He made the service of man to be itself the service of God. This is a vast advance from the immovable East. It is the Divine recognition of those energetic faculties which have especially marked the character of the Greek, the Roman, the German, and the Anglo-Saxon races of mankind. Christ has taught us how to be reverential, and serious, and composed. He has taught us no less how to be active, and stirring, and manly, and courageous. The activity of the West has been incorporated into Christianity because it is comprehended in the original character and genius of our Founder, no less than are the awe and reverence which belong to the East.

(2.) Again, in every Eastern religion, even in that

which Moses proclaimed from Mount Sinai, there was a darkness, a mystery, a veil, as the Apostle expressed it, a veil on the prophet's face, a veil on the people's heart, a blind submission to absolute authority. There was darkness around the throne of God; there was darkness within the temple walls; there was in the Holy of Holies a darkness never broken. To a large extent this darkness and exclusiveness must prevail always, till the time comes when we shall see no longer through a glass darkly. There always must be mystery in the greatest truths; "a boundless contiguity of shade," which no philosophy, no inquiry, no revelation, no decrees of councils, no speculation of theologians, can ever fathom or remove. This marks Christianity in common with all the religions of the East. But yet, so far as the veil can be withdrawn, it has been withdrawn by Jesus Christ and by His true disciples. He is the light of the world. In Him we behold with open face the glory of the Father. He came to bear witness to the truth. He went to and fro, rousing the hearts and the minds of men to seek for truth. In Him the cry of inquiry and of freedom which had already been awakened in the West found a ready response. Not without a purpose was the Greek language, with all its manifold flexibility, chosen for the vehicle of His teaching, rather than the stiff, immovable Hebrew. Not without a natural affinity did the Grecian philosophy attach itself to the first beginnings of the Gospel. Not unfitly were Socrates and Plato deemed by the early Fathers to have been Christians before the time. The revival of the studies of the ancient languages and the vast impulse given to the progress of human thought by the Reformation was in itself a new manifestation of Christ, a new declaration of His union with minds and classes of men who had before been deemed to be without God in the world. It is a constant reminder, that in using to the utmost the resources of science, in watching for light from whatever quarter, in sifting and searching all that comes before us to the very bottom, we are fulfilling one of the chief calls of our religion, we are accomplishing the very will of the Redeemer. Whatever is good science is good theology; whatever is high morality and pure civilisation is high and pure religion.

The freedom and progress of the West contrast as strongly with the stagnation of the East as the greenness of our fields contrasts with its arid plains, the shadows of our clouds and the freshness of our breezes with its burning suns, the ceaseless variety and stir of our teeming cities with its vast solitudes. And it is a contrast which Christ and Christianity have anticipated. It is God's gift to us, to be developed as our special contribution to the treasures of our common faith. Let us be of good heart, let us not be unworthy of our high calling. Wherever statements are received without evidence, wherever hollow watchwords are used like sounding brass and tinkling cymbal, there the shadow of barbarism is still upon us; wherever language is used as a veil to conceal our thoughts, wherever we allow ourselves to employ sacred words without meaning, there the light of the Gentiles has not dawned upon us. Truly it has been said, that the theological controversies which have agitated the Churches to so little practical purpose have turned on words which were not defined, and therefore not understood. The moment the words have been defined, and their meaning appreciated, that moment the excitement has cooled, and the passions evaporated. So it was with the scholastic disputes concerning the Trinity; so it has been with more recent disputes concerning Predestination and Justification. The spirit of Western enlightenment has turned its lantern upon them; and they have disappeared, or are disappearing, like phantoms and shadows, and the dayspring from on high has arisen in our hearts.

(3.) Again. There was in all Eastern religions, whether we look Godward or manward, a stern separation from the common feelings and interests of mankind. We see it, as regards man, in the hardness and harshness of Eastern laws; we see it, as regards God, in the profound prostration of the human soul, displayed first in the peculiarities of Jewish worship, and to this day in the prayers of devout Mussulmans. And this also enters in its measure into the life of Christ and the life of Christendom. The invisible, eternal, unapproachable Deity, the sublime elevation of the Founder of our religion above all the turmoils of earthly passion and of local prejudice—that is the link of Christianity with the East.

But, on the other hand, there was another side of the truth which until Christ appeared had been hardly revealed at all to the children of the older covenant. Degrading and erroneous as in many respects were the old Gentile notions of the Godhead, yet there was one thought which dimly and darkly ran through all the old religions of the nations which the Bible called the Children of Japhet: namely, the thought that the gods were not far removed from any one of us. They had from time to time come down into the ranks of men; they had been seen labouring, suffering, weeping, nay, even dying, for the service and the welfare of the human race. And this it is which in the life and character of Christ is wonderfully combined with that deep reverence for God of which the Eastern nations had received so large a share. In Christ we see how the Divine Word could become flesh, and yet the Father of all remain invisible and inconceivable. In Christianity we see not merely, as in the Levitical system, man sacrificing his choicest gifts to God, but God, if one may so say, sacrificing His own dear Son for the good of man. Not only the loftiness of God as with the Hebrews, but the condescension of God as with the Gentiles; not only the abasement of man as with the Jew, but the elevation of man as with the Greek—were in Jesus Christ set forth in indissoluble union. And with this closer revelation of the Divine compassion was called forth the justice, the gentleness, the mercy, the humanity, which the West has developed more strongly than the East, and which makes Christianity to be emphatically the religion of love and, in the largest sense, of charity.

These are some of the points in which Christianity combines the religion of the East and West — in which, having sprung from the East, it has become the religion of our Western civilisation. What do we learn from this? Surely the mere statement of the fact is an almost constraining proof that the religion which thus unites both divisions of the human race was indeed of an origin above them both; that the light which thus shines on both sides of the image of humanity is indeed the light that lighteneth every man. There is no monotony, no sameness, no one-sidedness, no narrowness, here. The variety, the complexity, the diversity, the breadth, of the character of Christ and of His religion, is indeed an expression of the universal omnipresence of God. It is for us to bear in mind that this many-sidedness of Christianity is a constant encouragement to hold fast those particles of it which we already possess, and to reach forward to whatever elements of it are still beyond us. Say not that Christianity has been exhausted; say not that the hopes of Christianity have failed, nor yet that they have been entirely fulfilled. "In our Father's house are many mansions." In one or other of these each wandering soul may at last find its place, here or hereafter.

I have spoken hitherto of the general contrast between the East and the West, between the Children of Shem and the Children of Japhet, between the sacred regions of Asia and the secular regions of Europe. I have tried to point out that here, as elsewhere, in the Gospel, that which was last has become first, that which seemed secular has become more holy than that which seemed most sacred; that the things of Cæsar are not separate from the things of God, and that by giving to Cæsar the things which are Cæsar's, we in that very act give to God the things which are God's. Thus far, what I have said is applicable to the whole Western world, on the other side of the ocean as well as on this side. In this respect we are all the common children of the mighty nations which formed the centre of the civilisation and history of mankind. But does not every word that has been uttered acquire a larger significance to a son of that Old World when, standing here for the first time, he looks upon this New World, of which, in their loftiest flight of fancy or inspiration, apostle or prophet never dreamed? Is it possible for him, as he descends from his flight on the wings of the morning, and lands on these shores, where the race and the faith of his fathers have struck so deep a root, not to feel again and yet again the thought which, more than a century ago, inspired the well-known line of the philosophic poet: "Westward the course of empire takes its way"? Far be it from any of us to pronounce with certainty that the latest offspring of time will be the noblest. Far be it from a stranger to forecast the duties or prospects which rise before his imagination, as he finds himself in this West beyond the West, in this West which even beyond itself looks forward to a yet farther West, towards which the bays and promontories of these eastern shores of the new continent shall, perchance, as the years roll on, stand in the same relation as the East, the ancient consecrated East, the ancestral hills and valleys of English and of European Christendom, stand to them. We cannot, we dare not, forecast the future; but we cannot, we dare not, repress the thought that a future, vast and wonderful for good or for evil, must be in store for those descendants of our common race to whom this mighty inheritance has been given. For the New World as for the Old World there is a glorious work to do, a work which requires all the reverence, all the seriousness, all the repose, of the East; all the activity, all the freedom, all the progress, of the West; all the long past of

Europe, all the long future of America—a work which neither can do for the other, but a work which both can do together.

"Hast thou but one blessing, my Father? bless me, even me also, O my Father!" This is the prayer which East and West, England and America, may well send up from shore to shore. Give to each the grace to learn from each. Give to each the strength to fulfil that pure and lofty mission which belongs to each. Give to each the spirit of wisdom and understanding, of "holy hope and high humility," to which the whole body of mankind, fitly joined together and compacted by that which every joint supplieth, according to the effectual working of every part, shall make increase of the body unto the edifying of itself in love. We have taken the wings of the morning, we have dwelt in the uttermost parts of the Western sea. O, may Thy hand even there lead us onward! O, may Thy right hand even there hold us up!

II.

THE HOLY ANGELS.

PREACHED IN ST. JAMES'S CHURCH, PHILADELPHIA,
SEPTEMBER 29, 1878.

"Thy will be done on earth as it is in heaven."—*Matthew* vi. 10.

It is on the last part of these words—"as it is in heaven," that I propose to dwell. We are invited to consider them by the festival of this day, Michaelmas. But there is no time or place in which we may not turn our thoughts from earth to heaven, from the seen to the unseen, from the confused, imperfect ways of the performance of God's will in this troublesome world to its perfect and Divine fulfilment in a better and higher state. It is on this that our thoughts shall now be fixed.

I do not propose to dwell at length on what is told us concerning the Holy Angels. It is not easy nor is it necessary, to separate what we have learned concerning them from the Bible, and what we have learned from the great representations of them in painting and in poetry. But the general idea which the belief in angels expresses is deeply rooted in the Christian heart and is full of instruction. If our thoughts concerning them are drawn more from Milton than from the Bible, yet Milton has, in his splendid imagery, laid hold of a noble doctrine, at once Biblical and philosophical. The idea of the heavenly host of angels includes the operations of God in the vast movements of the universe, and His ministrations through the spirits of men, whether now or hereafter. It includes that ideal world to which Plato fondly looked as the sphere in which reside the great ideas, the perfect images, of which all earthly virtue and beauty are but the imperfect shadows. It includes the thought of that peculiarly bright and lovely type of Christian character to which, for want of any other word, we have in modern times given the name of "angel" or "angelic"—superhuman, yet not Divine; not heroic, not apostolic, not saintly, yet exactly what we call "seraphic" or "angelic," elevating, attracting, with the force of inherent nobleness and beauty. "An angel's nature," says Luther, "is a fine, tender, kind heart, as if we could find a man or woman, who had a heart sweet all through, and a gentle will without subtlety, yet of sound reason. He who has seen such has seen colours wherewith he may picture to himself what an angel is." The idea belongs to that high region of thought where religion and poetry combine. Religious belief furnished the materials, but poetry wrought and transformed them into shapes which the latest religious culture of mankind can never cease to recognise. Let us, therefore, trace, so far as we can, the outlines of that perfect fulfilment of the Divine will of which here we see only the scanty and partial promise.

(1.) First, the will of God is perfectly done in heaven, because it is, as we believe, done with the unbroken, uninterrupted sense of the presence of God. It is well to know how to be in sympathy with the will of God; to feel truly the littleness of all that is little, and to feel no less truly the greatness of all that is great; to have a just measure of what is partial, secondary, indifferent, and of what is eternal, permanent, and essential; to look beyond the narrow present to the far-reaching past and future. This, which we may believe is the instinct of the blessed intelligences which stand around the throne of God, ought to be the aspiration, difficult and arduous, yet not impossible, of those who are struggling here on earth. "The Lord sitteth above the cherubim, be the earth never so unquiet." We should strive to look upon things on earth as we imagine that He looks upon them who sees their beginning, middle, and end. This is the first ground of the belief of which we are speaking.

(2.) Again, the thought of the host of heaven suggests the idea of order, law, subordination. When the most majestic divine of the English Church, Richard Hooker, was on his deathbed, he was found deep in contemplation, and on being asked the subject of his reflections, he replied "that he was meditating upon the number and nature of angels, and their blessed obedience and order, without which peace could not be in heaven; and oh! that it might be so on earth!" It was a meditation full of the same grand thought which inspired his great work on "Ecclesiastical Polity"—the thought of the majesty of law, "whose seat," as he says, "is the bosom of God, and whose voice is the harmony of the universe." The very words by which the angelic intelligences are described— "thrones, principalities, and powers"—the connection into which they are brought with the universal laws of nature—"He maketh the winds His angels, and the flames of fire His ministers"—bring before us the truth that by law, by order, by due subordination of means to ends, as in the material, so in the moral world, the will of God is best carried out. This truth gives a new meaning to those researches through which the students of nature are enabled, by working with those laws, to work out the will of their Maker. But it also gives a fresh force and interest to those other manifestations of law in the government of States or Churches, by which there also the will of God must be done on earth as by those higher laws in heaven; by the laws of duty in the human conscience; by the laws of nations; by the laws and constitutions which Divine Providence has, through the genius of man and the progress of arts, raised up in our different commonwealths. By such laws,

> the stars are kept from wrong,
> And the most ancient heavens through it are fresh and strong.

By such laws all human societies are kept from unruly disorder, popular violence, despotic tyranny. By the supremacy of such laws, has the Church and State of England hitherto been guarded and guided to temperate freedom, and wholesome doctrine, and solid unity. Out of such laws have sprung the great communities which trace their descent from England on this side of the Atlantic. And, oh! by the supremacy of law may we all continue to be ruled; by law may the passions of individuals be restrained, and the liberty of thought and of speech secured, and the peace and order of the whole community maintained! By such order and by such law may the whole of modern society, on this side of the ocean or the other, be maintained in the stress and strain now laid on every part of its complex organisation. Let justice, which is the soul of law, prevail, though heaven itself should fall; or, rather—as heaven cannot fall, if only justice be done—let justice, which is God's will in heaven, on earth have its perfect work.

(3.) Again the Scripture teaches—and our own heart and reason respond to the thought—that, combined with the universal sense of the Divine presence and of the Divine law, there is in the celestial world a wide diversity of gifts and operations. "Few and far between," indeed, are the glimpses which the Bible gives us of the heavenly hierarchy; yet they reveal to us such a variety of form and beauty as naturally befits the pattern and exemplar of this universe, so fearfully and wonderfully made, of this marvellous complexity of human souls and spirits created in one Divine image, though in a thousand types. The seraph's fire, we are taught to think, is different from the cherub's strength. We see the four living creatures before the throne, contrasted each with each, as ox with eagle, and eagle with lion, and lion with man; one star differing from another in glory; there a rainbow, like unto an emerald; there the guileless virgin souls following the gentle Lamb whithersoever He goeth; there the multitude, in white robes, with palms in their hands, that have come out of great tribulation; there the armed soldiers of heaven, galloping on white horses to victory.

Truly, "in our Father's house are many mansions;" truly, the gates of that heavenly city "are open continually, day and night." In those many mansions, through those open gates, by those diverse gifts, our Father's will is done in heaven.

It has been one happy characteristic of the Church of England, that it has retained these several aspects of the Christian character within its pale. There is in Westminster Abbey a window dear to American hearts, because erected by an honoured citizen of Philadelphia, in which these two elements are presented side by side. On the one hand is the sacred poet most cherished by the ecclesiastical, royalist, priest-like phase of the Church, George Herbert; on the other hand, the sacred poet most cherished by the Puritan, austere, lay phase of the Church, William Cowper. That diversity is an example of the way in which God's will is wrought on earth as it is in heaven. I have said that we do not speculate on the names or natures of angels, yet as symbols and outlines of the Divine operations they may be full of good suggestions. In the rabbinical and mediæval theology, this diversity used to be represented by the manifold titles of the various "principalities and powers." Most of these have now dropped out of use; but there are some few which, either from their mention in the Biblical or the apocryphal books, or from the transfiguring hand of artistic or poetic genius, have survived. Michael, the leader of the host of heaven, the champion of good against evil, the immortal youth of Guido's magnificent picture, trampling on the prostrate dragon; Gabriel, the pacific harbinger of glad tidings, the inspirer of heavenly thoughts, by whose gracious touch the greatly beloved Daniel was sustained, and the retiring Mary encouraged, to whom the Arabian Prophet in his cave looked for inspiration, to whom Milton assigned the delightful post of guarding the gates of the earthly paradise; Raphael, the "sociable spirit," the travelling companion of the good Tobias, the ideal of those angels whom, in mortal form, we sometimes entertain unawares, whose words, when ended,

> So charming left his voice, that we the while
> Think him still speaking, still stand fixed to hear;

Uriel, the "regent of the sun," "the light of God," seen for a moment in the books of Enoch and Esdras, but in Milton's poem the glowing representative of the angel of all knowledge; Ithuriel, the searcher, the discoverer of truth, with his spear whose touch of celestial temper no falsehood can endure; Abdiel, the everlasting example, as long as the English language lives, of courageous isolation, "the dreadless angel"—

> Among the faithless, faithful only he;
> Among innumerable false, unmoved,
> Unshaken, unseduced, unterrified.

Such are the Divine ideals that the angelic powers represent. They bring before us the summits of virtue, and also its divergences. As in heaven, so on earth let us strive, so far as is possible, that no light, of however a different a lustre from our own, be extinguished; that no strength of purpose or conscience, however diverse from our own, be shut out; that no aspiration after truth or duty, however wayward, be stifled; that no spark, even though it be that of the smoking flax, be quenched; that no soaring pinion be clipped in its upward flight; that, of all the many coloured shades, of all the numberless diversities, whether of English or universal Christendom, none be regarded as useless or worthless; that every good and perfect gift, whether in man or nature, whether in the Old World, with all its aged and venerable forms, or in the New World, with all its youth and vigour, be alike hailed as coming down from the "Father of Lights, with whom is no variableness, neither shadow of turning." Not in the exclusiveness of the courts of heaven, but in their width and openness, shall we rejoice hereafter: not by the exclusiveness of any Church or school on earth, not by the equality of all human characters, but by their inequalities; not by contraction within our own circle, but by our patient endurance of things beyond our narrow vision, ought we to rejoice now. "Every blessed spirit which ever existed"—so wrote one of the best of the Reformers to a prince bowed down by great bereavement, and asking anxiously concerning that unknown state beyond the grave—"Every blessed spirit which ever existed, every holy character which shall exist, every faithful soul which is living now, all these, from the beginning of the world even unto the consummation thereof, thou shalt hereafter see in the presence of Almighty God."

In that very diversity lies the strength, the beauty, and the interest of the celestial hierarchy. Nor was it without a deep meaning that the Book of Daniel speaks of "the angel"—the genius, as it were—of each particular empire and kingdom in the ancient heathen world. Those angel forms, those idealised representatives, the genius of each State, and Nation, and Church, still meet us in the commonwealths of modern times. Of these the whole family of Christendom and the whole family of mankind is composed. At the times when their characteristic diversities are most strongly brought out, we seem to see God's purpose in having allowed such diverse formations among His creatures. The angel of the old hemisphere, and the angel of the new hemisphere, are both dear in the sight of Him who made them both, and who designed for each a work which none but they, and they both separately and conjointly, can accomplish.

(4.) There is yet another thought suggested, especially by that name which gives its chief meaning to the festival of Michaelmas. "There was war in heaven; Michael and his angels fought against the dragon."

This is the ideal side of the greatest of earthly evils. There is war even in heaven, to carry out the will of God in casting out evil from the world; and so far as the same qualities are called forth by war on earth, it is true that even in the midst of the carnage of battle, even in the midst of the misery of precious lives lost, of brilliant hopes overturned, there is a likeness to the conflicts of the celestial hosts. Courage, self-control, discipline—these are the gifts by which victories are won on earth. Courage, self-control, discipline—these, if we may so say, are the gifts by which victories are won in heaven.

Some of us may have read the complaint uttered in one of the most striking works of American genius against the famous Italian picture to which I have alluded, in which the Archangel bestrides his fallen enemy in unstained armour, with fair, unfurrowed brow, with azure vest, with wings undisturbed. "Not so," says Nathaniel Hawthorne, "should virtue look in its death-struggle with evil; the archangel's feathers should have been torn and ruffled, his armour soiled, his robes rent, his sword broken to the hilt." Even in the contests of heaven there must be struggles, and of those struggles earthly warfare gives us a likeness and type. All honour to the efforts after peace which inspired the aims of that Society of Friends to which this city owes its existence, and yet it is not without significance that the only authentic portrait of William Penn is that which represents him in his early youth as a gallant soldier in complete armour, and with the motto, "Peace is sought by War." Peace, whether in religion or in politics, is the end, but it is often true that war and conflict must be the means. Michael the Archangel, the soldier of the heavenly hosts, is a true exemplar of Christian goodness, no less than the gentle Raphael or the gracious Gabriel. May God's will everywhere, and by all of us, be carried out with the same unswerving, persevering determination to resist and conquer evil by man's will on earth as by God's will in heaven.

(5.) Again, the heaven, where the Divine will prevails, is described in the Bible as a world of spirits. It is the spirit, the spiritual, which unites and vivifies the whole. In Ezekiel's complicated vision of the angelic operations of Divine Providence, it is the spirit which is in the midst of the wheels. "Whithersoever the spirit was to go they went, and they went every one straight forward, and they turned not when they went." In the vision of St. John, no less, all the worship is of the spirit, and of the spirit alone. "I saw no temple therein, and the city had no need of the sun or of the moon to shine in it, and there shall be no more curse, for the tabernacle of God is amongst them." Doubtless, in our imperfect state, the will of God cannot, in this respect, be done entirely on earth as it is in heaven. Yet still the thought of that state to which we all look forward helps us more clearly to understand what should be the aim and object of all earthly combinations and forms, whether of language, of government, or of worship. It is by the spirit, not the letter; by the essential substance, and not the accidental covering; by the better understanding of the meaning that lies beneath the words; by the better appreciation of unity amidst outward differences; by the comparison not only of earthly things with earthly, but of spiritual things with spiritual, without respect of persons or nations, that the unity of spirit, which is the unity of the blessed angels in heaven, can ever be produced amongst Churches or nations. Much of the course of this world may be carried on by colossal armies, and by blood and fire and sword, by gigantic commerce, by daring assertion of authority, by ceremonial observances, by dogmatic exclusiveness. But there is a higher course, which is carried on by the still, small voice of conscience; by the union of intelligent minds; by spirit, not by matter; by reason, not by force; by mind and heart, and not by external polity. Each one is, in this sense, a king to himself. The hosts which really govern the world are the thoughts and consciences of men. More dear in the sight of God and His angels than any other conquest is the conquest of self, which each man, with the help of heaven, can secure for himself. There is one great characteristic of the venerable religious society of which this city is the centre—namely, that alone of separate Christian communions it placed before it, as the object and reason of its existence, not any outward ceremony, not any technical doctrine, but the moral improvement of mankind—the insignificance of all forms and of all authority, compared with the inward light of conscience. This protest of the Friends, this lofty aspiration, may have been accompanied by many relapses, many extravagances, many glaring inconsistencies; but in itself, and looking not at its means, but at its ends, it is an example to all Christendom; it is not only Christian, but angelic.

(6.) There is yet one more aspect of this doctrine, the constant activity of the ministering spirits of God, in their care for His glory and for the welfare of men.

There are, indeed, those who serve, although they only "stand and wait;" those who in the temple of heaven, as in the temple on earth, do God's will by silent praise and contemplation. But this is not the usual description of the ministering spirits. They rest not, day nor night; their rest is in work, and their work itself is rest. They rejoice, so we are told, in the recovery of every fragment of good. And this ministration for our welfare extends even to those operations of Providence which seem at times most adverse. As in nature, the fierce rain, the wild wind, the raging fire, are often indispensable instruments for the purification of rivers, the invigoration of health, the reformation of cities, so also it is in individual experience. In our own lives how often it is that we come across what have been finely called "veiled angels."

> We know how radiant and how kind
> The r faces are those veils behind;
> We trust those veils one happy day
> In heaven and earth shall pass away.

There is one such veiled angel to whom, in Oriental countries, a special name has been given, well known through the words of a pathetic poem, taken as the motto of the most tragical chapter of English fiction. It is "Azrael, the angel of death." Yes, even Death, the darkest and sternest of the messengers of God, even he is, or may be, an angel of mercy. In a famous speech of one of our greatest orators during the European war of twenty-five years ago, there occur words which have never been forgotten by those who heard them, and which struck a sacred awe on the national assembly to which he spoke: "The angel of death is passing over the land. I seem even now to hear the flapping of his wings." Not only in war, but in every day of every year, in some household or other at this season, especially over the Southern region of this country, afflicted by wasting pestilence, that tread may be felt, the rustling of those wings may be heard. But the angel of death is also the angel of life, for if Death divides he may also reunite. The angel whose visits are of judgment and destruction invites and provokes us to works of charity and kindness. The angel who sits within the shadow of the sepulchre is also the angel of the resurrection of our immortal souls.

These then are the ways in which God's will is done in heaven:

First, the consciousness of the Divine presence;
Secondly, the majesty of law;
Thirdly, the diversity of Divine gifts;

Fourthly, the conflict with evil;

Fifthly, the spiritual character of the service of heaven;

Sixthly, the Divine beneficence.

May God grant that now and then—as we pray our daily prayers to God, for His will to be done on earth as it is in heaven—some one of these thoughts, so imperfectly expressed, may take possession of our souls.

III.

THE PERPLEXITIES OF LIFE.

PREACHED IN CALVARY CHURCH, NEW YORK, OCTOBER 6, 1878.

"Suffer me a little, and I will shew thee that I have yet to speak on God's behalf."—*Job* xxxvi. 2.

THE Book of Job is full of interest from beginning to end; its dramatic character, its pathos, pervade its structure throughout. It is divided into two sections. The first part describes, in the most vivid poetry, the misery and the hopes of the Patriarch. This occupies thirty-one chapters. But the pith and conclusion of the book is to be found in the second part, from the thirty-second chapter to the end. The long controversy of Job with his three friends is finished, when Job, although feeling that he was right, and they were wrong, breaks out into the cry: "Oh that one would hear me! Behold, my desire is that the Almighty would answer me." That cry was heard. The words of Job were ended; the three friends were silent; but there was yet another spectator drawn to the scene of sorrow—the youth Elihu. He had heard both sides; he had waited until they had all spoken, with that reverential deference which, in Oriental countries, marks the conduct of youth to age: but now he could restrain himself no longer. "He was full of matter, the spirit within him constrained him; he spoke that he might be refreshed." He opened his lips, and answered: "I am young, and ye are very old; wherefore I was afraid, and durst not shew you mine opinion. I said, days should speak, and multitude of years should teach wisdom. But there is a spirit in man, and the inspiration of the Almighty giveth them understanding. Great men are not always wise, neither do the aged understand judgment. Therefore I said: Hearken to me; I also will shew mine opinion." He then, with trembling and hesitating accents, in confused and complicated arguments, entreats them to listen to him, for he speaks in and for a higher power than his own. "Suffer me a little, and I will shew thee that I have yet to speak on God's behalf."

Some critics have thought that the character of Elihu was introduced into the book at a later date, in order to clear up the perplexed horizon; but, at any rate, his part forms an integral element in the sacred story as now handed down to us. It is like that of the wise chorus in the Grecian tragedy; like that of an impartial judge balancing the arguments of a contested cause. Gently and calmly, without vehemence, and without anger, he turns the attention of the Patriarch from himself and his sufferings to the greatness, the power, the wisdom of God. The complaints of Job against his friends might be right, but "against God—behold in this they were not just." "I will answer thee, that God is greater than man. Why dost thou strive against Him? for He giveth not account of any of His matters." And thus he rises to a strain yet higher; he leaves the comparison of good and evil in this life, and turns to the purer and clearer works of God in creation. Then there comes the final confirmation of his view of the world: "While Elihu yet spake, his heart trembled and was moved out of its place;" there was a roar of thunder and a whirlwind, and from the whirlwind the Lord answered Job and said: "Who is this that darkeneth counsel by words without knowledge?"

The wonders of nature were unfolded piece by piece before his face; "the laying of the foundations of the earth, when the morning stars sang together;"

the waves of the sea, the sun, the planets, the snow, the clouds, the mighty forms of the animal creation, the marvellous instincts of beast and bird, the warhorse impatient for the battle, "Behemoth" (that is, the hippopotamus) revelling in his unwieldy strength, "Leviathan" (that is, the scaly crocodile of the Egyptian Nile). What the hard dogmatism of the friends had been unable to effect, is now at last impressed by the terrible yet glorious vision of the Divine works in creation. Before that solemn display of the majesty of God the proud spirit of the ancient chieftain was bowed down, and he said: "I know that Thou canst do everything, and that no thought can be withholden from Thee." "I have heard of Thee by the hearing of the ear, but now mine eye seeth Thee; wherefore I abhor myself, and repent in dust and ashes."

This is a brief summary of the close of this instructive book. Let us draw from it its chief practical lessons. They are four in number; four lessons, as we may call them, on the perplexities of life.

(1.) First, the wisdom put into the mouth of Elihu, when the three friends had failed, recalls to us the truth taught elsewhere in Scripture, that there are times when traditional authority must give way, when he who is young may instruct those who are aged, when "out of the mouths of babes and sucklings God has ordained" that very "strength" which the world most needs. That deference to age and experience on which the three friends insist, is indeed the general rule both in sacred and common life. Unless it were so, society would always be dissolving and reconstructing itself afresh; teaching and acting would lose that solidity and stability which is the only guarantee of progress as well as of permanence. Hesitation and modesty are the true models of youthful reverence at all times. But the doctrine which is shadowed forth in the appearance of Elihu is this, that each generation must learn not only from that which has gone before, but from that which is coming after it. The rising generation, for what we know, has some truth which the older generation may have failed to apprehend. Even a child can instruct its elders, by good example, by innocent questions, by simple statements. Elihu "was young," and the three friends "were very old;" yet to him, and not to them, was entrusted the message of pointing out the true answer to the great difficulty which had perplexed them all. It was indeed no new truth which he put before them; but it was, for that very reason, the more needed that the quick and lively eye of youth should rightly perceive it and apply it. So to put forth old truths that they may with each successive age wear a new aspect; so to receive new truths that they may not clash rudely with the old; this is the function which God entrusts to each new generation of mankind. So, again and again,

> God hath fulfilled Himself in many ways,
> Lest one good custom should corrupt the world.

So, again and again, new life has been breathed into expiring systems, new meanings into ancient creeds, new applications have been given to the most venerable truths. The younger nations are called to take charge of the older races. A new world, as our English statesman said, is called into being to redress the misfortunes of the old. Let not that new world fail of its mission from any narrowness of view, or darkness of insight, or false shame, or false presumption.

(2.) Secondly, the Book of Job impresses upon us that there are problems beyond the power of man to exhaust; and in that certainty of uncertainty it is our privilege to rest. The human mind, it has been well said, may and ought to repose as calmly before a confessed and unconquerable difficulty as before a confessed and discovered truth. The error, both of Job and of his friends, had been to think that they could measure the counsels of God, that they could determine the course of His judgments: the friends declaring that because Job was afflicted he could not be righteous; Job complaining that, because he was righteous, he ought not to be afflicted. Elihu, on the other hand, and the voice from the whirlwind, taught that "touching the Almighty we cannot find Him out;" "He is excellent in power and justice, and in plenty of judgment; He will not afflict without need." In that power and justice and judgment, no less than in His mercy and love, let us place our absolute confidence. "God," as the old proverb says, "never smites with both hands at once;" with one hand He strikes to afflict, but the other is uplifted behind the veil, to bless, to heal, and to purify. We may rest assured that the Supreme Mind has a purpose, even though we do not see it.

And how is this truth enforced on Job? It is by the unfolding before him of the wonders of the natural world. To him, as to all the ancient Gentiles, "the invisible things of God, even His eternal power and Godhead," would be chiefly seen through the creation of the world, through the things which are made. To us a deeper revelation has been vouchsafed; and were another Elihu to appear before us to confirm our faith, it would not only be from the wonders of nature, but from the "still small voice" of the Gospel and of the Spirit, which tells us that in the life and death of Jesus Christ the will of God and the duties of man are for ever united. The cross of Christ is the pledge to us that the deepest suffering may be the condition of the highest blessing, the sign, not of God's displeasure, but of His widest and most compassionate love. But though we have thus been raised above the need of Elihu's ancient mission, yet still the description of the natural world is often the best guide to us, as to Job; and the more, because our view of nature is so much fuller than it could be in the days of the Patriarch. To the primeval ages of the world, the fiery horse of the wilderness, the monsters of the river Nile, were more wonderful, and are therefore in this book more largely described even than "the sweet influences of Pleiades," or "the bands of Orion;" even more than "the watercourse, or the overflowing of the thunder." But to us, who have been taught the immeasurable distances, the incalculable magnitude, of the heavenly bodies, which to Job seemed only twinkling points in the firmament of heaven; who have been taught the wonderful system of the movements of cloud and storm, which in those older times must have seemed to be separate shocks and isolated convulsions; to us the argument in the closing speeches of the Book of Job is strengthened a hundredfold. We know that what we see are but the outskirts of creation; that the power and the wisdom which rule this vast universe must be beyond the reach, not only of our understanding, but of our furthest speculation. Many a one who has been perplexed by the uncertainties and contentions of history, has been strengthened by the certainty and the unity of science. "The moral perversions of mankind would have made an infidel of me," said one of the best prelates of this century, "but for the counteracting impression of a Divine providence in the works of nature." Whatever else the discoveries of modern science teach us they teach us this—the marvellous complexity and the unbroken order of the material world; they indicate to us, how vast is the treasure-house of resources by which the immortality of each separate spirit, the inter-communion of spirit with spirit, and of all with God, may be sustained in a higher world. They confirm the thought that "now we know in part, and see through a glass darkly," but that in the infinite immensity in which God dwells, and into which we hope we may pass after death, "we shall know even as we are known."

A famous English philosopher, dear to the Western world—Bishop Berkeley, whose footsteps, whose relics, and whose name the traveller follows with interest at Newport,* at Hartford,† at Yale,‡ and even to the shores of the Pacific §—has described a comparison which occurred to him in St. Paul's Cathedral in London, as he saw a fly crawling up one of the pillars: "It required," he says, "some comprehension in the eye of an intelligent spectator to take in at one view the various parts of the building, in order to observe their symmetry and design; but to the fly, whose prospect was confined to a little part of one of the stones of a single pillar, the joint beauty of the whole, or the distinctive use of its parts, were inconspicuous, and nothing could appear but the small inequalities on the surface of the hewn stone, which, in the view of

---

* In the house called "Whitehall," the rocks called "Paradise," and in Trinity Church, at Newport.
† His chair is in the college at Hartford.
‡ His legacy of books is in the library at Yale.
§ The new college at San Francisco is, I am told, called after Berkeley's name.

that insect, seemed to be so many deformed rocks and precipices." That fly on the pillar is indeed the likeness of each human being as he creeps across the vast pillars which uphold the universe. That crushing sorrow, which appears to us only a yawning chasm, or a hideous obstruction, may turn out to be but the jointing or the cement that binds together the fragments of our existence into one solid whole. That dark and crooked way, through which we have to grope in doubt and fear, may be but a curve, which, in the sight of superior intelligences, shall appear to be the tracery of some elaborate ornament or the span of some majestic arch. Everything which enables us to see how the universe is one whole; everything which shows that man is bound by subtle links with all the other parts of creation; everything which shows us how many of the miseries of the world of man, the wretchedness of improvidence, intemperance, and sensuality, are also breaches of the fixed rules of nature; everything which confirms us in the belief that the revelation of the Infinite and the Divine is not confined to a single race or Church, but pervades, more or less, all the religious instincts of mankind; everything which impresses upon us the continuity, the unity of the Divine and human, of the sacred and secular, brings us into the frame of mind which the Bible and experience alike impress upon us as needful for the reception of the first principles of true religion.

(3.) This brings us to the third lesson contained in the Book of Job. "I abhor myself," says the Patriarch, "and repent in dust and ashes." He was called away from dwelling on himself, and on his own virtue, to feel that he was in the presence of One before whom all earthly goodness and wisdom seemed insignificant. It was the same truth to which the friends had vainly endeavoured to bring him, but to which they could not bring him, because they combined it with a contradiction against which his conscience and reason revolted.

He had been right in the assertion of his own innocence; his friends had been wrong in believing that his calamities were judgments on his sins. Still he was at last brought to confess that "though he had whereof to glory, yet not before God." Looking at himself, not in comparison with other men, but in comparison with the All-holy and the All-pure, his sufferings seemed to assume another aspect. "God is in heaven, and we upon earth; let Him do as seemeth Him best." Those upon whom the tower in Siloam fell were not sinners above the rest of mankind, but all such calamities warn us to take a serious and solemn view of our mortal condition. They bring us into the presence of Him, before whom we feel that sense of sin and infirmity which we naturally shrink from expressing in the presence of our fellow-men. When we think of Him as He appeared to Job in the works of creation, when we think of Him from whom nothing is hidden, and in the light of whose countenance our secret sins are set, it is no mock humility, but the simple expression of our most enlightened conscience, to abhor ourselves before Him, and repent in dust and ashes.

A pious old Churchman of the last generation, Joshua Watson, used to say that as life advanced his abhorrence of evil in himself and his loathing for it so increased, that in his latter days confessions of sin, which in youth had seemed to be somewhat exaggerated, became the sincere voice of his heart.

No doubt there is another instinct in human nature, the very reverse of this, the consciousness that we are made in the image of God, that we are the masters of our own destiny, the heirs of all the ages, crowned with glory and honour, some of us with the faculties, all perhaps with the hopes of angels. It was the glory of one of the great religious teachers of New England to have brought out this feeling with a force which, even if exaggerated, has left an enduring mark on his age, which neither in Europe nor America can easily be effaced. It is part of the buoyancy and elasticity of mind which is so remarkable a heritage of this people, and which gives so strong a pledge of their future greatness.

Yet still, the self-abasement of Job is not the less a necessary element of that perfect and upright character, of which he is represented as the type.

And not only in moral matters, but in intellectual matters also, do we learn this need for humility. How often do we hear ignorant, half-educated men, how often do we hear audacious young men, pronouncing on difficult problems of science and religion with a certainty which to those of mature years seems absolutely ridiculous. We all have need of the grace of humility. We have need of the conviction that many of us, perhaps most of us, are but as dust and ashes in the presence of the great oracles in the various branches of knowledge that Divine wisdom has raised up amongst us. We have need of willingness, of eagerness to be corrected by those who fear to tread where we rush boldly in, and of a desire to improve ourselves by every light that dawns upon us from the past or the present, from the east or from the west, from heaven or from earth.

(4.) Lastly, the sense of the vastness of the universe, and of the imperfection of our own knowledge, may help us in some degree to understand, as in the case of Job, not, indeed, the origin of evil and of suffering, but, at any rate, something of its possible uses and purposes. We look round the world and we see cruel perplexities—the useless spared, the useful taken; the young and happy removed, the old and miserable lingering on; happy households broken up under our feet, disappointed hopes, and the failure of those to whom we looked up with reverence and respect. We go through these trials with wonder and fear; and we ask whereunto this will grow. But has nothing been gained? Yes, that has been gained which nothing else, humanly speaking, could give. We may have gained a deeper knowledge of the mind of God, and a deeper insight into ourselves. Truths which once seemed mere words, received without heed and uttered without understanding, may have become part of ourselves. In time past we could say, "We heard of God by the hearing of the ear," but now we can say, "Our eye seeth Him." Humility for ourselves, charity for others, self-abasement before the Judge of all mankind, these are the gifts that even the best men, and even the worst men, may gain by distrust, by doubt, and by difficulty.

May I close these words by an illustration drawn from the lips of a rough seafaring man, one of the few survivors of a great wreck which took place some years ago, when a crowded steamship foundered in the stormy waters of the Bay of Biscay? As soon as those who had escaped from the sinking vessel found themselves in a small boat on the raging sea, they discovered that their chief danger came, not from the massive sweep of the waters, but from the angry breaking waves which descended upon them from time to time, and against which every eye and hand had to watch with unabated attention. As the shades of evening grew on, the survivor who told me the story said that his heart sank at the thought that in the darkness of the night it would be impossible to see those insidious breakers, and that sooner or later the boat would be engulfed by them. But with the darkness there came a corresponding safety. Every one of those dangerous waves, as it rolled towards them, was crested with phosphoric light, which showed its coming afar off, and enabled the seamen to guard against it as carefully as if they had been in full daylight. The spirits of the little company revived, and though, from time to time, the cowards or the desperadoes amongst them were for turning back, or driving an oar through the frail boat's side, the coruscations guided them through the night; and they did at last, in the early dawn, catch a view of the distant vessel by which they were saved. That crest of phosphoric light on the top of those breaking billows was as the light of Divine grace, the compensating force of Providence, in the darkness of this mortal night, and on the waves of this troublesome world. The perplexity, the danger, the grief, often brings with it its own remedy. On each bursting wave of disappointment and vexation there is a crown of heavenly light which reveals the peril, and shows the way, and guides us through the roaring storm. Out of doubt comes faith; out of grief comes hope; and "to the upright there ariseth up light in the darkness." With each new temptation comes a way to escape; with each new difficulty comes some new explanation. As life advances, it does indeed seem to be as a vessel going to pieces, as though we were on the broken fragments of a ship, or in a solitary skiff on the waste of waters;

but so long as our existence lasts we must not give up the duty of cheerfulness and hope.

> The sense that kept us back in youth
> From all intemperate gladness,
> That same good instinct now forbids
> Unprofitable sadness.

He who has guided us through the day may guide us through the night also. The pillar of darkness often turns into a pillar of fire. Let us hold on though the land be miles away; let us hold on till the morning break. That speck on the distant horizon may be the vessel for which we must shape our course. Forwards, not backwards, must we steer—forwards and forwards, till the speck becomes a mast, and the mast becomes a friendly ship. Have patience and perseverance; believe that there is still a future before us; and we shall at last reach the haven where we would be.

IV.

THE USES OF CONFLICT.

PREACHED IN THE CATHEDRAL OF QUEBEC, OCTOBER 20, 1878.

"Who is this that cometh from Edom, with dyed garments from Bozrah? this that is glorious in his apparel, travelling in the greatness of his strength?

"I that speak in righteousness, mighty to save.

"Wherefore art thou red in thine apparel, and thy garments like him that treadeth in the wine-fat?

"I have trodden the wine-press alone, and of the people there was none with me: for I will tread them in mine anger, and trample them in my fury; and their blood shall be sprinkled upon my garments, and I will stain all my raiment. For the day of vengeance is in my heart, and the year of my redeemed is come."—*Isaiah* lxiii. 1-4.

THIS passage belongs to that second portion of the Book of Isaiah in which the Prophet is anxiously looking forward to the return of his people from the Babylonian captivity. He supposes himself to be at Jerusalem, and he describes that he sees a figure advancing from a distance, advancing from the south, from the red mountains where dwelt the old hereditary enemies of Judah, the children of the red-haired Esau, who, in the day of the destruction of Jerusalem, had said: "Down with it, down with it, even to the ground!" His form is terrible to behold. His robes are scarlet, as with the vivid colour of the rocks of Petra, from whence he comes—Petra, "the rose-red city"—crimson as the cliffs from which the fastness of Bozrah looks down over the Promised Land. "Who is this that cometh from Edom? with dyed garments from Bozrah? this that is glorious in his apparel, 'tossing back his head' in the greatness of his strength?" And from the far-off conqueror comes the gracious answer: "It is I that speak 'of righteousness,' I that am mighty to save"—I, who not only speak of what is right and true, but come, at all hazards, to do it, and carry it on to victory.

Once again the Prophet gazes on those blood-red garments, as their colour flashes more distinctly on his view. He sees that they are not, as they seemed in the distance, the scarlet mantle worn by the warrior chiefs of the Arab tribes, but rather like the raiment of those who, in southern and eastern countries, enter the wine-press at the vintage, and with naked feet crush the purple clusters, and press out the juice of the grape, till they wade knee-deep in a foaming crimson torrent, which dashes, as in waves and fountains of blood, over the clothes of the treaders. "Why art thou red in thine apparel, and thy garments like him that treadeth in the wine-fat?" And the answer comes once more: "I have trodden the wine-press alone, and of the people there was none with me. For I trod them down in mine anger, and trampled them in my fury; and their blood was sprinkled on my garments; and I have stained all my raiment. For the day of vengeance is in mine heart, and the year of my redeemed is come." The retribution was at last to fall on the savage tribes of Edom; the crisis of their fate was surely to approach, and Israel was no more to be vexed by their insolent triumph; a bright era was to open before the chosen people, as when their ancestors had marched through these mountains into their place of destined rest.

Such is the literal occasion of the prophecy, and it is in part suggested by the like denunciations of vengeance against Edom in the thirty-fourth chapter. It is one of the instances in which Hebrew prophecy repeats itself from century to century; the later prophet taking up and applying what the earlier prophet had first uttered.

The vision, as we see, reflects in the deepest dye

what may be called the sanguinary character of ancient Jewish history. It is one of the few visions, almost the only vision, of this kind in the utterances of the Evangelical Prophet. It breaks in upon the peaceful melodious strains of his salutations and consolations like a thunder-clap in a clear sky, like the clash of arms in a bridal feast. It breathes throughout the deep undying hatred of the race of Jacob towards the race of Esau, roused to the utmost pitch by the ungenerous delight which the Edomites had taken in the fall of their ancient rival. It is the concentration of the cry for vengeance which runs through the brief prophecy of Obadiah, and which closes with a sunset of blood the tender delicate pathos of the hundred and thirty-seventh Psalm. It lent its imagery to that same fierce sentiment continued in after ages by the Jewish people, when the name of their dead enemy Edom was transferred to their living enemy, the Roman Empire; and yet again when Christendom began those cruel persecutions of the Jewish race which ought still to raise a blush of shame on every Christian cheek, when the soul of Esau was believed by Israelite Rabbis to live over again in the Churches and States of Europe, and echoes, not loud but deep, of the curses of the ancient prophets still rang in many a synagogue, in many a house of traffic, in Rome and in Toledo, in Venice and in York.

So regarded in its first historical meaning, the prophecy belongs to that outward vesture of Divine things which waxeth old and is folded up; deeply instructive in its relations to the history of the ancient Jewish race, but on that very account with no permanent bearing on the fortunes of Christendom or of mankind. But the more keenly we figure to ourselves this external difference, the more fully do we perceive the significance of the inward spirit which gives to this, and other like words of Jewish prophecy, an enduring value. Edom has passed away. Whether it received its death-blow from the Maccabees or the Romans, the race of Esau no longer haunts the rocks of Petra or the fortress of Bozrah. Other nations have peopled these lonely fastnesses. The maledictions of the prophets as regards this particular object have exhausted themselves ages ago. But not so the principles which lie at the root of those maledictions— like a pearl, as a well-known interpreter of prophecy said, "like a pearl at the bottom of the deep sea."

There are, we may say, when we examine this prophecy, two such principles—one of more limited, and one of more universal application. The more limited application is that which arises out of the question: What was the source of this bitter, inexpiable hatred against the race of Edom? It was this. The enmity of Edom, unlike the enmity of Babylon or Nineveh, was not the attack of open foes in fair fight; it was the destruction of friends by friends; it was the desertion of kinsmen by kinsmen; it was the crime of hounding on the victorious party, of "standing by on the other side" in the day of the sorest need of the weaker or the vanquished cause. This is no obsolete evil confined to ancient days. The wicked old proverb, "Howl with the wolves," is a maxim which is still but too common—a maxim as hateful to the Christian evangelist as it was to the Hebrew prophet. The prophecy in this sense breathes the true chivalry of human nature, of Christian nature. It calls upon us all, old and young, to remember that to trample on a fallen foe, whether in public or in private life, is neither wise nor generous.

But there is a more general truth involved in the very sound of the heart-stirring words, a bracing and invigorating note, as though we heard the voice of a trumpet talking with us. What is this universal truth? It is that good is achieved in this mixed world of ours chiefly by struggle and combat. There is always the red range of Edom to be surmounted before we can reach the Promised Land; there is always the wine-press to be trodden before we drink the juice of the grapes; there is always the battle to be fought before the victory is won. It is not enough to speak of righteousness; we must be active in doing it. It is not enough to wait till others help us; we must act and fight, we must do and dare, though we stand alone—though "of the people there be none with us." We may look, and there will be none to help; we may wonder that there is none to uphold; but a just cause is its own support; our own arm, in the strength of God, may bring salvation to us; the fury, righteous passion, indignation, enthusiasm of a single man is enough to uphold a sinking cause.

Let me take some particular instances in which this general principle is established.

First, let me speak of the most sacred of all its exemplifications. These words are not, indeed, in any strict sense of the phrase, a prediction of our Saviour's coming. They are never quoted as such in the New Testament. They have no historical reference to His life. But they are something much more than a prediction. They are a *prophecy* in the strict sense of the word—that is, an announcement of a Divine truth, of which the historical manifestation of Jesus Christ was the chief end and the crowning example. Not in the letter but in the spirit, and yet partly even in the letter, the thrilling question of the Prophet might have been repeated when the people of Jerusalem stood round the open space on Calvary, and saw approaching up that mournful way a figure "whose visage was marred more than any man, and his form more than the sons of men." His garments were red with blood; His very sweat was as it were great drops of blood falling down to the ground. "Who is this that cometh from Edom, with dyed garments from Bozrah? . . . Wherefore art thou red in thine apparel, and thy garments like him that treadeth in the wine-fat?" So it might well be asked, in accents of awe mingled with grief; and the answer is the same as to the Prophet: "I that speak of righteousness, and am also mighty to save." Yes, that mean, that despised, that blood-stained, that agonised form is the form of the Invincible Conqueror. He has not only been the Prophet, the Teacher of righteousness; He has also been mighty to put His words into deeds, His promise into performance. He is alone. His friends and disciples have fled. He has trodden the wine-press alone, and of the people of His age there was none with Him. But in the midst of this isolation He is still the King of Kings and Lord of Lords, acknowledged as the foremost figure of human history, as the clearest personification of the Divine perfections. His own arm has brought salvation to Him. His strong love, strong as death, hath upholden Him. "For the day, not of vengeance, but of forgiveness, is in His heart, and the year of His redeemed is come." Out of that dark hour and that fierce agony, was destined to be brought the redemption, the civilisation, the sanctification of mankind.

The same general truth which lies expressed in the vision of the conqueror of Edom, in the sufferings of Christ, can also be seen in many vicissitudes of human life. Let us look at it as it regards individuals. We are here guided by the application of this prophecy in Scripture itself. Look at the visions in the Apocalypse,* where the older language is worked up again in a new form. Look at that vision of the heavenly warriors following their heavenly Leader on white horses as He rides before them with His vesture dipped in blood. Who are they? Who are those celestial champions of Christendom who come in the thickest fray to help those that have no helper? There

---

* *Rev.* xix. 11-16.

are the martyrs for the early Christian faith, who literally came with their garments dyed in blood, the advanced guard, the forlorn hope, who fought their way through the passes of Edom for us and for themselves, witnesses to the sacredness of conscience, and to the value of a noble and honourable death. There, too, are the martyrs of truth and science, who, in solitary study, misunderstood, neglected, and unrequited, have trodden the wine-press of knowledge alone; or who—like the earliest explorers and discoverers of these regions, who fixed the first European habitation on this spot —laboured that other men might enter into their labours, and enjoy the Land of Promise, which they only saw in the far futurity, as from the top of Pisgah. There, too, are the firm companions and friends of our youth and age—faithful through good report and evil, who appear at the right moment, like guardian angels at our side, warding off temptation and misfortune, encouraging us when there was no one else to encourage, warning us when there was no one else to warn, advising us in spite of ourselves, standing by us when the world turned against us. There, also, is the young boy or the young man, at school or college, doing what he knows to be right, avoiding what he knows to be wrong, remembering what he has learned at home, though far away. There, too, are the pure-minded and high-spirited amongst men, who stand perhaps alone in a frivolous, selfish circle, yet still holding their own against the ridicule of foolish enemies or the flattery of false friends—determined to work, though their neighbours are idle; to be frugal, though those around are extravagant; to be truthful, pure, and temperate, though those around are treacherous and self-indulgent.

And again, there is another vision in the Apocalypse* in which the same figure is taken up with a still profounder meaning: "What are these which are arrayed in white robes, and with palms in their hands, and whence came they? These are they which came out of great tribulation, and have washed their robes, and made them white in the blood of the Lamb." That is to say: These are they who have suffered, not only in temptation, but in the innumerable sorrows, disappointments, mortifications, and changes of this anxious pilgrimage of life. These are they who have been refined and purified in that long struggle; who have learned from their own sorrows and from their own trials to feel for the sorrows and the trials of others; who have gained

* *Rev.* vii. 13, 14.

through that experience a power beyond their own—the power of faith, the power of sympathy, the power of rising above the petty cares of earth, the power of discernment between what is solid and enduring and what is false and fleeting. Truly that blood in which their white robes are washed is the blood of the Lamb—not the blood offered to appease an angry God, but the life blood (the blood which is the life) of the gentle and spotless Lamb; the drops of that same agony which watered the Garden of Gethsemane, filling up, as the Apostle says, the afflictions of Christ, who was tempted like as we are, and learned wisdom like us by suffering.

And if this great law of Divine redemption be true of individuals, if struggle and suffering be their condition of good, and if that good be thus the key to much that is mysterious in the suffering and the struggle, so also it is in regard to the more complex affairs of nations and Churches.

Alas! if we look over the history of the world, how often it seems but one vast blood-red field, one long ascent of Calvary. "Who is this that cometh from Edom, with dyed garments from Bozrah?" "Wherefore art thou red in thine apparel, and thy garments like him that treadeth in the wine-fat?" Is not this the description of the human race itself? Is it not the aspect as of a bleeding warrior emerging from a hard-won fight, splashed with the gore of the slain, plume and helmet crushed, sword broken, and armour bruised? When we look on the desolation of war, its necessary horrors, its unnecessary but too often concomitant sins—Can any good, we are sometimes tempted to say, come out of this Edom, this Golgotha, this vast confusion of misery? For what end has been this waste of blood, of energy, of precious lives, of noble souls, of high intelligence? Often, indeed, in the course of human history, we must say with grief, None— none whatever. In one sense they belong to that outward frame of old Hebrew prophecy, that dismal imagery of vengeance and destruction and carnage, which Christ came not to fulfil but to destroy. But, nevertheless, here also the inward principle of the prophecy still holds its course. There is something even in the remembrance of former wars, something in the very heat of the turmoil of civil or national conflicts, which braces our nerves, which clears the atmosphere, which dispels frivolity, which restores a just balance of things important and things trivial, which compels us to look into ourselves, which sifts and tears to pieces the false pretences and false arguments of every party.

There is something also in the profession of a soldier which keeps alive before the world the inestimable value of some of the greatest Christian virtues—courage, discipline, and honour. A soldier's temptations may be beyond the temptations of other men, but for that very reason the example of a good soldier, pure, and just, and noble-minded, is beyond all other examples a city set on a hill, a fortress that cannot be taken, an encouragement to the weak and wavering everywhere. In the midst of that burning fiery furnace of war there appears a Divine Form walking with us; we know not whence He came, or how He is there, but He will at last prevail, if only we have grace to recognise Him, to seize the opportunities which, out of these excandescent heats, fly off as sparks from the anvil. As iron sharpeneth iron, so is man to man. War and conquest are amongst the woes of God's heaviest judgments, but how often have the finest and noblest results grown out of it! How vast has been the moral impulse given to national life by such struggles, whether from within or from without! Look at the history of this famous place. How closely has the memory of later years bound together the names of the two heroic rival chiefs who perished on the same day, almost in the same hour, beneath the walls of Quebec! How strong an incentive to the best and most generous feelings of human nature is the joint tribute which we all involuntarily pay to Wolfe and to Montcalm! And, again, how singular is the providence which, out of those long conflicts between England and France on these Western shores, has worked out the peculiar result of this Dominion of Canada, where the language and the manners of the two great civilising races of Europe flow together, as hardly anywhere else, in one harmonious stream, and sustain the influence and image of the ancient monarchies of Europe, side by side with the great republic of this New World.

And, again, if the principle of the ancient prophecy applies to the turmoils of the State, no less is it true of the turmoils of the Church. There again, as we look at the divisions of Christendom at large, or of any one of its separate Churches, the question often arises, Who is this that cometh from Edom with garments dyed in Christian blood—the seamless raiment rent in twain by the violence of Christian controversy? Can this be the Prince of Peace? Can this be the God of Love? Can this be the Merciful and the Just? Yet here, also, is another side to the picture. Here, also, must the Truth of God enter into its rest by hard-won victory, by generous rivalry, by the eager conflict of soul with soul and mind with mind. Union of the same elements is nothing; it is only the union of diverse elements which makes unity worth having. If all were the eye, where were the hearing? and if all were the ear, where were the seeing? We may have absolute agreement and sameness—every face like every other face, every mind like every other mind; but we should then have none of the variety of nature, none of the culture of civilisation, none of the richness and the fulness of Christianity. But in proportion as any Church is civilised, and national, and comprehensive, there must be divisions, and those very divisions are the sign of comprehension and of vitality. As in the State, so in the Church, it is by argument, by debate, by the intercourse of different souls, that truth is sifted, and light struck out, and faith tried, and charity perfected. There are streams of religious thought which, like the Nile, can diffuse beneficence by their sole strength, without tributary or accessory aid; but the stream of the highest Christian truth, in this respect, resembles the mighty river, the glory of the Western world, which flows beneath the heights of Quebec, and which derives its force and majesty from that peculiar conformation of this continent which has made it the depositary and the outlet of all that vast volume of waters which, in hidden springs, and immense lakes, and world-renowned cataracts, discharge themselves into its broad channel, and make it the highway of the nations. Such is true Christianity, accepting and including all the elements of life which, from the inland seas of far antiquity, or the rushing torrents of impetuous action, or the dissolving foam of ethereal speculation, find their way into its capacious bosom.

No doubt, whether in the Church or the State, there is a sense in which these divisions may become our destruction instead of our edification. There is a sense in which a house divided against itself cannot stand; in which the river of life may be so swelled as to burst its bounds; and that is when these divisions become embittered by stupid prejudice, by personal malignity, when each exaggerates the faults of each, when each looks upon each, not as an element of life to be included, but as an element of death to be thrust out. That indeed is Edom without Palestine, Golgotha without Redemption, the Crucifixion without Christ.

But there is a more excellent way by which differences lead to counsel and to strength. It is the comparison of truth with truth, the candour which fair discussion engenders, the generosity which springs from matured knowledge, the conviction which springs from honest doubt, the determination to see the meaning which lies behind the words, to seek in different practices and doctrines not their worst, but their better side.

"Who is this," we may once more ask, "that cometh from Edom—that is glorious in his apparel, travelling in the greatness of his strength—leading his people through the deep, as a horse through the wilderness, that they should not stumble?" It is indeed CHRIST Himself. It is the Spirit, the Eternal Spirit, of His life, and of His death, of His acts, and of His words. It is those who see in Him something vaster and higher than any single Church, or than any single leader, who see in Truth something greater than any one of the particular forms of Truth; who see in love and charity something grander even than faith or hope, even than agreement in opinion, even than uniformity in worship. Such as these may, with their Master, tread the wine-press alone, but not the less have they the future in their hands; and in the faith which breathes this spirit, however imperfect, however struggling, they will stand fast for ever, because it has in it the pledge of immortality, because the day of victory is in its heart. The blood with which they are sprinkled is not the blood of fierce conflicts, nor yet even the blood of which I have before spoken, wrung out by suffering, whether in ourselves or in others. It is the blood of Christ in that highest sense in which it is used in the Bible—not merely the blood of His agony, but the life-blood of His Spirit, which alone gives force and virtue to all His efforts for us; the life-blood of Christ and Christendom, which is love or charity— the love which sees in the service of man the best and highest means of the service of God.

We have spoken of all the various manifestations of principle which the text involves, and we have travelled far away from the blood-stained vision of the Prophet to more peaceful and homely applications of the general truth, that the good of man and the will of God can only be carried out by long struggle and exertion.

Is there not an exemplification of this truth present with peculiar force at this moment? The whole city of Quebec, the whole Dominion of Canada is lamenting at this moment the departure of perhaps the most beloved and valued ruler who has ever swayed its counsels. Or, if this be too much to affirm when we think of those who have gone before, yet at least we may say that he who yesterday took his last farewell of these shores showed us in his high position what are the special qualities by which rulers have made, and can make, themselves beloved and valued by those whom they are called to govern. This is not the place, nor would it be fitting for me, to speak of those peculiar graces and gifts which enabled your late Governor to carry out so successfully his exalted mission. But there is one aspect under which his example was applicable, not only to all statesmen, but to all conditions of life. Not by the conflict of war or struggle, but by that pouring out of the very life-blood of a generous nature, was the work accomplished and the recompense attained. Whatever gifts he had were all used to the uttermost for the public service. Whatever graces of art or speech had been given to him by nature, were made available for the sake of rendering those around him and beneath him happy, and at ease, and useful. No stone was left unturned that could by him be turned for this object; no time, no labour was spared that could forward the work that was to be done. These are homely arts, but they are arts often neglected. For the want of them the wheels of the world's progress drag heavily; by the use of them the course of civilisation and religion runs smoothly onward. They are arts, too, which in our humble measure are within the reach of all. Each can use his talents, whatever they may be, with that ungrudging devotion for the public good which was employed in the use of those loftier talents in that high place. Each can make the little world around him more happy and more useful by determining to despise and ignore what is base and trivial, by resolving to make the best and the most of all that there is of good, and noble, and generous, whether in ourselves or others. May we all show our grateful sense of him whom we have lost by doing likewise ·each· in our sphere. May the successor, who in a few weeks will take his place with the most sacred pledge which the Sovereign of England has yet given to these distant possessions, in like manner devote the energies of his noble and ancient race, and the purity of his blameless life, to the fulfilment of the great task entrusted to him. May he and she, when their work is closed, depart with the like reward of a grateful people, with the like consciousness that they too have used to the utmost the greatness of their strength; that they too have moved forward the hours of the eternal year of redemption from all evil, and of advance towards all good.

www.ingramcontent.com/pod-product-compliance
Lightning Source LLC
Chambersburg PA
CBHW020258170426
43202CB00008B/427